Southern Living

Home Lighting

Oxmoor
House.

Southern Living® Home Lighting was adapted from a book by the same title published by Sunset Books.

Consulting Editors: Don Vandervort, Jane Horn
Editorial Coordinator: Vicki Weathers

Senior Editor: Jim McRae
Assistant Editor: Jennifer Ormston
Art Director: Odette Sévigny
Writer: Stacey Berman
Researcher: Adam van Sertima

Special Contributors: Lisa Anderson, Andy Brown, Linda Cardella Cournoyer, Jean-Guy Doiron, Lorraine Doré, Martin Francoeur, Dominique Gagné, Sara Grynspan, Robert Labelle, Rob Lutes, Jennifer Meltzer, Ned Meredith, Jacques Perrault, Jacques Pomerleau, Edward Renaud, Jean Sirois, Jennifer-Lee Thomas, Jean Warboy, Judy Yelon

Book Consultants:
L.T. Bowden, Jr.
Kevin Heslin

Cover
Design: Vasken Gulragossian, James Boone
Photography: Langdon Clay
Interior Design: Charme Tate

Our appreciation to the staff of *Southern Living* magazine for their contribution to this book.

First printing January 1999
Copyright © 1999 by Oxmoor House, Inc.
Book Division of Southern Progress Corporation
P.O. Box 2463, Birmingham, Alabama 35201
All rights reserved, including the right of reproduction in whole or in part in any form.

Southern Living® is a federally registered trademark of Southern Living, Inc.

ISBN 0-376-09062-6
Library of Congress Catalog Card Number: 98-87047
Printed in the United States

CONTENTS

THE BASICS OF GOOD LIGHTING

A well-lit room is one in which all the planning and technical details, and even the light fixtures themselves, blend to create a seamlessly beautiful effect, allowing your eyes to focus on the objects the light falls upon rather than on the light itself.

Lighting can dramatically affect a room's atmosphere and comfort level, so it's important to consider, whether you're modifying an existing home or building a new one. An essential element of good lighting design is common sense: The best lighting schemes put light just where it's wanted and needed.

In this chapter, we'll discuss some of the principles of good lighting, how to work with the architectural features of your home, and what types of light fixtures are available. Once you have some ideas in mind, you may want to contact a lighting designer or other design professional, for advice or a complete plan, depending on your project and budget. In the end, your personal style and needs will be your best guide.

Custom wall sconces and candles lead the way down this hallway to the living spaces beyond. Incandescent strip fixtures along the tops of the beams bounce ambient light off the warm wood of the raised ceiling, creating a contrast to the rich blue skylight colors.
**LIGHTING DESIGN: LINDA FERRY
ARCHITECT: DAVID MARTIN, AIA
INTERIOR DESIGN: JOHN SCHNEIDER, ASID**

ELEMENTS OF LIGHTING DESIGN

Good lighting design can provide the right amount of light for the various activities that take place in a room, allow different users to control light levels to their own preferences, and minimize energy consumption without compromising comfortable light levels.

For design help, there are various professionals available. Lighting designers are trained in creating home lighting schemes; architects and interior designers also have various levels of skill and experience in this area. If you use the services of more than one professional—an architect and a lighting designer, for example—they should work together to create a unified design. If you choose to do the job yourself, a little imagination and some basic lighting know-how will serve you well.

TYPES OF LIGHTING

Lighting designers separate electrical lighting into three categories: task, accent, and ambient.

Task lighting: Used to illuminate the area where a visual activity—like reading, sewing, or preparing food—occurs, task lighting is often achieved with individual fixtures that direct light onto a work surface.

Accent lighting: Similar to task lighting in that it also consists largely of directional light, accent lighting is primarily decorative. Use it to focus attention on artwork, highlight architectural features, or set a mood.

Ambient lighting: Also called general lighting, ambient lighting provides a soft level of light appropriate to such activities as watching television or entertaining. Ambient lighting may come from fixtures that provide a diffuse spread of illumination. A directional fixture aimed at a wall can also provide a soft wash of light.

In addition to electrical light, using daylight to provide ambient light and even task lighting is becoming more popular. Daylight can be harnessed with strategically placed skylights and windows. It's a great way to conserve energy, at least during daytime hours. To control heat and glare, you may require special window glazing and shading. Consult a window manufacturer or a professional designer for advice for your situation.

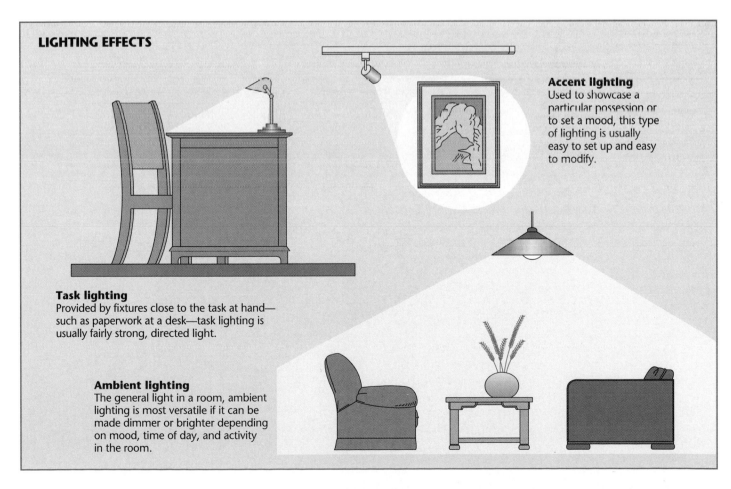

LIGHTING EFFECTS

Accent lighting
Used to showcase a particular possession or to set a mood, this type of lighting is usually easy to set up and easy to modify.

Task lighting
Provided by fixtures close to the task at hand—such as paperwork at a desk—task lighting is usually fairly strong, directed light.

Ambient lighting
The general light in a room, ambient lighting is most versatile if it can be made dimmer or brighter depending on mood, time of day, and activity in the room.

APPROPRIATE LIGHT LEVELS

Comfortable light levels are a matter of individual preference. Some people who work in brightly lit offices grow accustomed to this kind of environment and want the same level of light in their homes. Others prefer relatively low light levels, with higher levels of illumination primarily in areas where they're reading, working, or relaxing.

For many years, North Americans have lived in relative brightness indoors—common light levels have been much higher than those in Europe, for example. But concern for energy conservation has scaled down recommended light levels, creating a trend toward bright lighting in task areas and softly lit surroundings.

FACTORS THAT AFFECT LIGHT LEVELS

When you're determining how much light is needed for a given activity, weigh these factors:
• The difficulty of the task to be performed;
• The speed and accuracy with which it must be done;
• The color contrasts among the materials involved;
• The eyesight of the person engaged in the activity.

As we age, we require higher levels of light outside the eye for the same amount of light to reach the retina, the part of the eye where the light receptors are located. For example, an older person performing a visually demanding task, such as embroidery, will usually require more light than someone younger performing the same task. A dimmer, a three-way bulb, or two

---

MEASURING LIGHT LEVELS

Light emitted by a source (light bulb) is measured in lumens. If you look at the sleeve around a light bulb, you'll see that it states both the bulb's wattage, the amount of electricity used by the bulb, and the number of lumens, the amount of light, that the bulb produces. But lumen output is not a very useful measure for calculating light levels in a room, because it only indicates how much light the bulb produces. It doesn't tell you how much light gets past the lamp shade or how much of it reaches the surface you're interested in lighting. A better indicator is footcandles, a measure of the amount of illumination provided by one lumen over a surface one foot square.

Experts measure footcandles with a special meter, but you can measure them using the light meter of a manually adjustable 35mm camera and the conversion chart at right, top. To find the number of footcandles of light reaching your kitchen counter, for example, place a large sheet of white paper or cardboard on the counter at a 45° angle. Set the camera's ASA meter at 100 and the shutter speed at 1/30 second. Without throwing a shadow on the card, line up the card through the camera's viewfinder and adjust the f-stop to the proper exposure for taking a picture. Use the table above, right, to translate your f-stop reading into the approximate footcandle level.

Some standard recommended footcandle levels for various household tasks are shown in the chart at right, bottom. The high number is recommended for difficult tasks or for older people; the low number is for easier tasks or younger people. Of course, these are only recommended levels. You may find that more or less light is needed.

CAMERA LIGHT METER FOOTCANDLE READINGS

F-Stop	Footcandles
f2	10
f3.5	15
f4	20
f4.5	30
f5.6	40
f6.3	60
f8	80
f9	120
f11	160
f14	240

RECOMMENDED FOOTCANDLES

Activity	Footcandles
Entertaining	10-20
Dining	10-20
Casual reading	20-50
Grooming	20-50
Kitchen, laundry—general light	20-50
Kitchen—food preparation	50-100
Prolonged reading or study	50-100
Workshop activities	50-100
Sewing, medium-colored fabrics	50-200
Sewing, dark fabrics	100-200
Hobbies involving fine detail	100-200

fixtures on separate switches will allow you to fit the illumination level to the people and task involved.

GENERAL LIGHT LEVELS

Though providing enough light for task areas is of primary importance, you also need to properly light the surrounding areas with accent light, ambient light, or both. If these areas were not at least softly lit, whenever you looked up your eyes would have to compensate for a dramatic change in light levels between the task area and the rest of the space—this could eventually result in eyestrain.

COLOR RENDITION

Different light sources contain different wavelengths of color. For example, incandescent light includes colors from most of the spectrum but has a large proportion of yellow and red. When dimmed, incandescent light becomes even more red. The color appearance of a light source, called its correlated color temperature, or CCT, can be described by its position on the Kelvin (K) scale. Lights with CCTs below 3100K are reddish or warm and lights with higher temperatures are increasingly blue.

A light's color affects how we perceive the color of objects on which it shines. For example, the color of a blue vase under a bluish light will be heightened as the light's color intensifies the vase's color. Under a reddish light, the same blue vase will appear dull and grayish, because the red light waves are absorbed, and there are no blue waves to be reflected by the vase.

Not all lights with the same correlated color temperature affect our perception of color in the same way. Under some lights, certain ranges of color may seem distorted or appear unnatural. Light bulbs and tubes are assigned a color rendering index, or CRI, based on how natural colors appear under them. As CRIs increase to the 80s and 90s, color rendition improves, meaning colors will appear more natural.

A light source's color rendering ability is important for home lighting, because it affects how furnishings, decorating materials, and even people will look. Incandescent lights, which we're used to having in our homes, have CRIs in the 95 to 100 range. Older-

Curved cabinets and counter lines are repeated in a cold-cathode ceiling cove in this kitchen (right). Low-voltage downlights give accents, and undercabinet fluorescents add task light. Besides their color options and efficiency, cold-cathode sources are quite flexible, as they can follow many shapes and dim to almost no light output.
LIGHTING DESIGN:
CAROL DEPELECYN,
CHRISTOPHER THOMPSON
(TALIS, INC.)
ARCHITECTS:
BILL GAYLORD AND WILLIAM
CASTILLO (GGLO)
DESIGN:
CAROLLYNE COBY
(DESIGN 5)

style and lower-quality fluorescent lights may have CRIs around 62 and may have cooler CCTs, which together usually make them unacceptable for home lighting. High-quality fluorescent lights, especially those in which the tube is coated with triphosphors, also called rare earth phosphors (usually designated RE), have CRIs of 80 and over. This is an acceptable level for home lighting applications, particularly for ambient lighting. To get an idea of the effect of different CRIs, visit a lighting showroom; many will display a variety of light sources, making the process of comparing colors and light easier.

REFLECTANCE

How the color and texture of the walls, ceiling, and floor of a room contribute to the general light level depends on their reflectance—that is, the degree to which they reflect the light shed on them.

Colors containing a lot of white reflect a larger amount of light and darker colors absorb light. For this reason, if you were to redecorate your living room by covering creamy white walls with a rich blue wallpaper, you'd need more light sources or higher-wattage bulbs to get the same light level as before. On the other hand, to maximize light levels without adding any additional electrical light sources, paint walls and ceilings a light color or white. In a room with light-colored walls and ceiling, light is distributed farther and more evenly, and reflected from surface to surface, until it gradually diminishes.

Texture plays a less important role in reflectance than color does. Matte finishes diffuse light; smooth, glossy finishes bounce light away, reflecting it onto other surfaces. Thus, in a room with fabric- or paper-covered walls, you'll need more light to achieve the same light level as in a room with painted walls.

BALANCING AND LAYERING LIGHT

To ensure an attractive, comfortable lighting scheme, you'll need to think about balancing light—creating an effective spread of weak and strong light throughout the room. The key to balancing is in layering light. First determine the focal point or points of the room, and give these areas the brightest light. Having two or three focal points is usually best, and sometimes areas of primary and secondary focus are established. A middle layer of light provides interest in specific areas without detracting from the focal points and a final layer adds light in the background. Of course, this is a design guide; not all layers of light are needed in all situations.

The first two layers are usually met with task or accent lighting (page 5), depending on what is being lit. The remaining light is ambient light, perhaps provided by an overhead fixture, wall sconces, or a soffit light. The contrast between the different intensities of light in the room should not be too great. Designers plan on a ratio of about 5 to 1 or at most 10 to 1 between the brightest light in the room and the fill light. Higher ratios are too uncomfortable for everyday living. See page 6 for information on measuring light levels.

Dimmers and control panels, available at lighting and hardware stores, and home improvement centers, can help you custom-tailor light for multiple uses and decorative effects. Dimmers enable you to set a fixture or group of fixtures at any level, from a soft glow to full throttle, and can save energy by allowing you to reduce a light's output. Control panels allow you to monitor multiple functions from one spot.

AVOIDING GLARE

One of the most important considerations in the placement of light fixtures is avoiding the possibility of glare. Direct glare—a bare light bulb—is the worst offender. When positioning fixtures, consider typical sitting or standing positions around the room, and make sure the bulb is not visible from them. Deeply recessed fixtures or fixtures with baffles or pinhole apertures will help remedy the problem, as will clip-on louvers and shutters, like those shown on page 17. The interior surface finish of the reflector can also affect the amount of glare.

Watch for reflected glare, too. Light bouncing off an object into your eyes is a hidden concern. Light reflects off an object at the angle at which it hits it. If light beams hit a surface at 20°, for example, they will leave it at 20°. If the angle is too steep, the light produces a hot spot, which can warp delicate surfaces, or be uncomfortable for someone sitting in its path for too long. A range of about 30° to 45° is comfortable; see page 12 for an illustrated example.

If a fixture is located directly over a flat, shiny surface, such as a dining room table, veiling glare can pose a problem. You can place nonreflective objects on the table to deflect this glare, or add a dimmer to the fixture so that the light level can be reduced until it's comfortable.

LIGHTING YOUR HOME

Once you have an understanding of basic lighting principles, you can consider how to apply them in your home. The first steps toward improving your home's lighting involve careful consideration of the design and layout of your rooms, as well as the types of activities that take place in each room.

It's a good idea to make a basic sketch of the layout of the room. Draw your plan to scale and note the location of major furnishings. These sketches will help determine where to place the light fixtures and the best kinds to use. You'll also be able to decide on the best location for new receptacles or switches.

MULTIPURPOSE LIGHTING

When working on a lighting plan, you'll find that some areas—including hallways, stairs, entries, closets, and workshops—host only one type of activity. Lighting these areas is relatively simple; often, one level of light and one set of fixtures is sufficient.

Living rooms, great rooms, and other multiple-use areas present more of a challenge. Users of these rooms may be engaged in activities as diverse as reading, entertaining, watching television, or practicing a musical instrument. Light levels required for these activities range from soft ambient light to strong task lighting.

Since all of a room's specialized lights will not be needed at once, one way to accommodate many activities in the same space is to plan for a variety of light levels, sources, and controls. For example, if model-building or working on puzzles is enjoyed at a table that doubles as a snacking area when you're entertaining, you might choose a pendant fixture with a strong light controlled by a dimmer; the high wattage can be used for task lighting, and the dimmer can be applied during entertaining.

An adjustable floor lamp or short track system above the piano can light both sheet music and the surrounding area when your piano student is at work. For reading or sewing, you can place a table or floor lamp with a three-way bulb next to an easy chair. See page 13 for more on light fixtures and their uses.

Table lamps for task lighting, downlights for both accent and general lighting, and the occasional fire for ambiance turn this elegant den (left) into a flexible space where a variety of activities can take place.

HIGHLIGHTING ARCHITECTURAL FEATURES

Light can both complement the special architectural features in a house and help to disguise some aspects you'd like to downplay. Use your room plan or walk through the house to help you focus on where lighting effects could be helpful.

Room dimensions: You can use light to play tricks with lighting dimensions, making small rooms appear open and airy or large rooms cozy and inviting.

In a small room, washing the walls with an even layer of light seems to push them outward, expanding the space. If the wall is light colored, the effect is greater.

A large room illuminated with a few soft pools of light concentrated on important objects or areas appears smaller and more intimate, as the lighted areas demand more attention than the room as a whole.

Narrow rooms benefit from creative lighting, too: lights along shorter walls draw the eye away from long ones, resulting in a seemingly wider space.

Ceilings: If your ceilings seem too low, bounced indirect light from uplights, torcheres, or coves can have the effect of raising them. On the other hand, to make uncomfortably high ceilings seem closer, keep light off them. Use downlighting, from surface-mounted (not recessed) or pendant fixtures.

Downlighting can also help downplay ceilings with rough or patchy plaster, a common problem in older homes. Draw attention to beautiful cathedral or beamed ceilings with uplighting from coves or well-placed spotlights. Beamed ceilings are often a good place for track lighting, since the beams can disguise the tracks.

Windows and skylights: Sources of daylight, windows and skylights can pose problems at night, when they seem like dark mirrors or black holes if left uncovered.

Bright diffusing lamps or fixtures can produce an annoying glare and reflection in a window. One way to avoid reflections is to light the area outside the win-

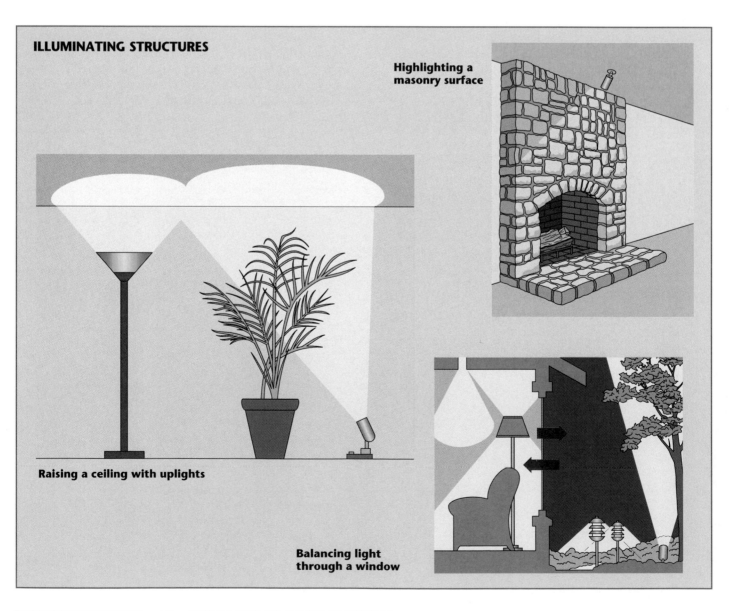

ILLUMINATING STRUCTURES

Highlighting a masonry surface

Raising a ceiling with uplights

Balancing light through a window

dow, to help balance light levels inside. This use of outdoor lighting visually extends the living area after dark. Another solution is to use opaque pendant fixtures or recessed downlights. If properly aimed, only the lighted areas will then be seen, not the light sources.

For skylights, fixtures concealed behind diffusing panels can offer the feeling of continuing daylight, and eliminate the dark hole effect.

Mirrors: Lighting mirrors can be tricky. Ideally, position the light to shine on people in front of the mirror, but make sure that it won't shine into their eyes. Lighting the mirror itself creates an interesting effect, but keep in mind that the mirror may reflect the fixtures—this might be unattractive or cause glare.

If there's no wall space for fixtures, you can mount wall sconces or strip lights directly on the glass. In a bathroom, try a fluorescent tube along the mirror top. Choose a high-quality light with good color rendering properties *(page 7)*.

Masonry surfaces: Play up the textures of brick walls, stone fireplaces, and other masonry surfaces by lighting them from an angle. Experiment to find the angle that works best for your situation.

Solar rooms: A large bank of windows on the south or west side of a solar room calls for artificial light elsewhere in the room, to counteract the contrast between the brightness of the sunlight and the shadows which the sun produces.

DECORATIVE ACCENTS

Permanent architectural features influence lighting plans, but so do the more movable, decorative aspects of your home. Furniture placement, art display, and even plants can make a difference in the placement, quality, and quantity of light needed.

Furniture arrangement: In any given area, certain lighting needs are dictated by the furniture arrangement. For example, you may want wall fixtures above your buffet for serving and for ambient light, or you may want a

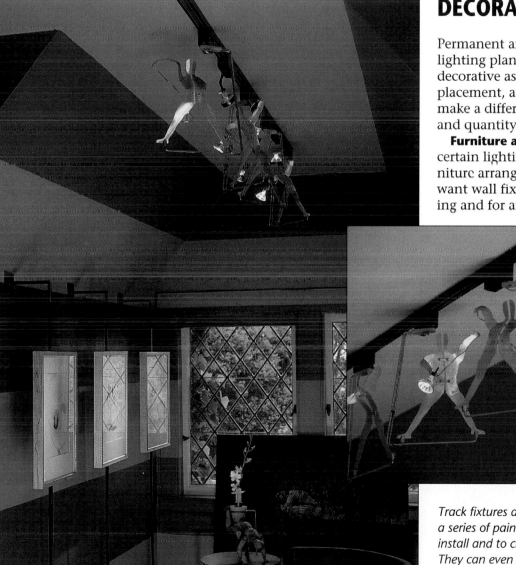

downlight to shine into a freestanding wardrobe, to make clothing selection a little easier.

Artwork: For the most dramatic effect, spotlight works of art individually from above or below. A 30° angle is best—even less if you wish to play up the texture. Track lighting will allow you to illuminate more than one piece

Track fixtures are traditional choices for accenting a series of paintings or collectibles—they're easy to install and to change as your displays change. They can even be part of the display, like these "little metal men" that turn simple low-voltage track fixtures into whimsical works of art. Designer fixtures like these are available from design firms and select outlets.
Design: David Turner and John Martin (Turner Martin)

at a time. Fixtures should be as close as possible to the piece, respecting manufacturers' specifications. To avoid wasting light, and therefore energy, you'll want a beam spread that lights all of the object and as little of the wall around it as possible. Select low-voltage fixtures when possible, for even greater energy savings.

Frame-mounted picture lights are another option, though these may not illuminate a painting uniformly. Washing the wall in light evenly from above will provide enough ambient light to see the pictures, but will not make the pictures a focal point.

Sculptures and other three-dimensional objects usually call for lighting from both sides to minimize shadows. To emphasize the shadows, or create a silhouette, aim a single spotlight at the sculpture from behind or below. Don't hesitate to experiment to achieve the results you want.

Collections: Lighting requirements for collections vary. Books and records are best lit evenly; other items may require individual spotlighting. Light panels or fluorescent tubes produce the most even glow; canisters and mini-tracks are best for accenting.

Downlighting may result in top shelves casting shadows on those below. Backlighting, vertical lighting from the sides, or lights attached under the front edges of shelves will eliminate this problem.

Concealed fixtures help keep glare out of people's eyes and lend a clean look to your display. See the illustrations below for more on lighting collections.

Indoor plants: To grow well, and to look their best, indoor plants need light. Some plant lovers use one watt of incandescent light for every three watts of fluorescent light; a more convenient solution is to purchase special "grow bulbs," available in specialty shops.

Attractive plants can be silhouetted with concealed uplights, or backlit against a luminous panel or lighted wall. Wall-mounted fluorescent fixtures provide even light for plants or potted trees.

FILLING IN DARK AREAS

Once task and accent lighting is taken care of, ambient lighting should be considered. It can be used to soften the contrast between bright areas of light and the surrounding spaces. For more, see the section on appropriate light levels on page 6.

Ambient light can be simple to obtain—it can come from a diffused or dimmed fixture or lamp, for example. As well, ambient light can be achieved using more creative solutions, including valances over curtained windows, fixtures bounced off the ceiling or walls, or indirect shelf or display-niche lighting. Uplighting—from torcheres or built-in coves—can create an especially subtle touch in living areas. Remember to direct bright light away from common standing areas.

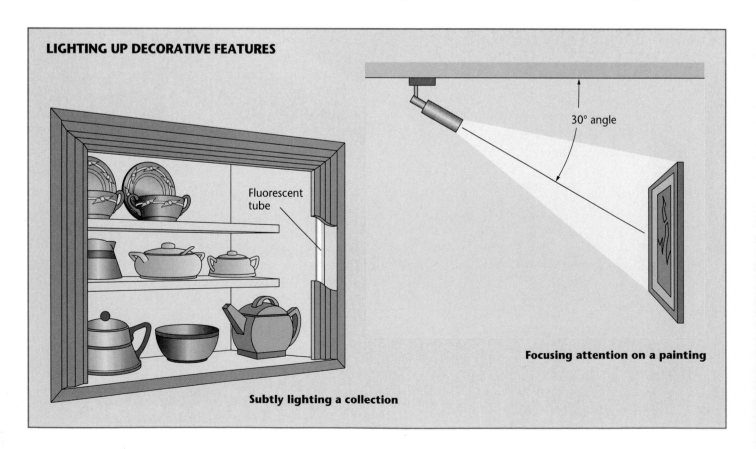

LIGHTING UP DECORATIVE FEATURES

Fluorescent tube

30° angle

Focusing attention on a painting

Subtly lighting a collection

SELECTING LIGHT FIXTURES

Once the quality and quantity of light needed for your home has been determined, purchasing the light fixtures is the next step. Lighting, hardware, and electrical supply stores are all good places to start.

Before you buy anything, observe the lighting in locations such as restaurants, stores, or a neighbor's house. Look for practical examples of the many different types and uses of lighting, then try to narrow down the effects that would suit your home, room-by-room. A lighting designer or other professional is another good source of advice. With your needs and preferences in mind, you'll be better prepared to hunt for the fixtures that provide the type of lighting you want.

Your choice may be influenced by the properties of the bulbs or tubes that will go in the fixture. Turn to page 19 for information on bulbs and tubes.

STANDARD-CURRENT VERSUS LOW-VOLTAGE LIGHT SYSTEMS

Standard-current lighting systems are installed in most homes. Many fixtures and accessories available on the market are catered to this system.

Because they're safer, more energy-efficient, and easier to install than standard 120-volt systems, low-voltage lights have become very popular indoors, as well as out. Such systems use a transformer to step down standard household current to 12 volts. There are packaged low-voltage systems available, or you can create your own system with individual fixtures.

Whatever lighting system you choose, remember that there are procedures and regulations to consider when extending and adding wiring routes. Contact your local building department or refer to the *National Electrical Code* branch circuit requirements for more on planning, installing, and maintaining light systems.

CHOOSING THE FIXTURES

Once you've formed some ideas about the kinds of lighting you need, selecting fixtures would appear to be easy. But given the great variety available today, finding the right fixtures can be confusing and complicated. Here are some points to keep in mind.

Function: Lighting systems should include fixtures that give strong directional light, general diffused light, or a combination. One of the primary considerations about any fixture is how it directs the light. For example, does it create a narrow, focused beam of light, a broad, diffuse spread, or something in between, like the torchere shown at right? For greatest efficiency, match the fixture's light distribution pattern to the lighting need.

Size: Fixtures will often appear smaller in the store than they will in your home. Take measurements of your top choices; then hold bowls or boxes of the same sizes in place to evaluate the scale. Manufacturers often produce fixtures in graded sizes, so ask about other sizes.

Design: Personal taste plays an important role. As well, professionals have found that a sense of decorative continuity can be created by using similar fixtures throughout a home. Manufacturers offer families of fixtures which include spotlights, pendants, tracks, and ceiling lights.

Cost: When calculating costs, there's more to consider than the price of the fixture.

The energy consumption of the bulbs or tubes that will go in the fixture is also a significant factor—fluorescents are more efficacious (produce more light per watt) than incandescents, leading to potential savings on your electricity bill. Also, some fixtures are more efficient than others, transmitting a higher percentage of the light produced by the bulbs or tubes they contain and, therefore, providing more light for the amount of electricity consumed.

More expensive fixtures usually offer more flexibility and higher quality. In some circumstances, you may find that having more control over the light may be worth the extra cost.

Flexibility: Tastes, habits, and styles change over the years. Your lighting system should be flexible enough to accommodate these changes. Movable or adjustable lamps are of course very flexible. But track systems and even built-in down lights can be changed, too. You can move fixtures along a track or change the way they're aimed and transform a regular built-in downlight into a pinhole light or an eyeball with a change of trim.

Maintenance: To operate efficiently, all fixtures should be cleaned regularly. Kitchens, bathrooms, and work areas demand fixtures that are easy to reach and clean. For hard-to-reach areas, such as above the stairs, a fixture with a long-lived fluorescent bulb is a good choice.

INDIRECT LIGHTING FIXTURES

Also called architectural or built-in fixtures, indirect lighting fixtures are often a good choice for ambient lighting and sometimes for task lighting. Simple and architectural in design, these devices usually consist of fluorescent tubes attached to the wall or ceiling and shielded from view. Light spills out around the shield and can be somewhat directed (up, down, or both) by the position of the shield relative to the tubes. Added accessories *(page 17)* can shield the tubes from view.

The initial cost of the fixtures, tubes, and wiring may be higher than for a standard incandescent floor lamp, for example, but the long life of the tubes and their energy efficiency usually pay off in the long run.

Built-in fixtures have different names, depending on how the light is directed. Coves and soffits perform opposite functions: Coves direct light upward onto the ceiling, while soffits spread light below. A soffit used at the top of a wall unit or bookshelf will direct

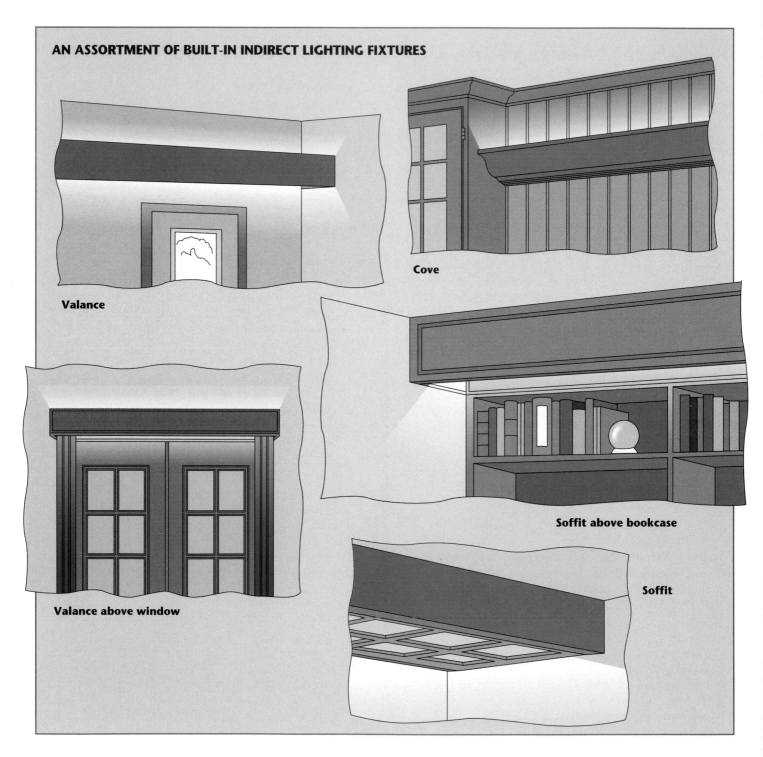

AN ASSORTMENT OF BUILT-IN INDIRECT LIGHTING FIXTURES

Valance

Cove

Valance above window

Soffit above bookcase

Soffit

light down onto the display. Valances send light both up to the ceiling and down over the wall.

Architectural fixtures can also be used for task lighting. A soffit or valance over a desk or kitchen counter-top, for example, may provide sufficient light. Like any fixture that washes a wall or ceiling with light, architectural fixtures will highlight surface imperfections such as uneven surfaces or taping irregularities.

RECESSED CEILING FIXTURES

Recessed downlights, another type of built-in fixture, offer light without the intrusion of a visible fixture. For this reason, they're particularly effective in rooms with low ceilings or sleek lines. Essentially a dome with a light bulb set in the top, a recessed downlight can be fitted with any one of a number of trims that aim the light to fit the function desired.

When used over sinks and countertops in kitchens, an open downlight spreads strong task lighting over the work surfaces. Open fixtures are also good for lighting stairways and entries.

Equipped as a wall-washer fixture, a recessed downlight throws light onto a nearby wall. A series of such fixtures can be used for even, balanced lighting of bookcases, for example, or to provide ambient lighting. Adjustable eyeball or elbow fixtures are good for highlighting objects on a wall.

The appropriate distance from the wall for a fixture depends on the fixture itself. Manufacturers will specify an acceptable range. Generally, fixtures grouped together should be spaced as far from each other as they are from the wall. For wall washing, fixtures are typically mounted in a series about 3 feet away from the wall to be washed, with 3 feet of space left between fixtures.

Low-voltage downlights—especially those with MR-16 bulbs and black baffles—are very popular for accent lighting. Low-voltage downlights may include an integral transformer, or you can use one external transformer to serve a number of fixtures.

Recessed fixtures can be added in existing ceilings, provided there's enough space between the ceiling and the floor or roof above. Fixtures range from $5\frac{1}{4}$ inches to more than 12 inches in depth, though some manufacturers offer shallower models for use in tight spaces. If you're installing a fixture in an insulated attic floor, get one that is safe for use with insulation; check the manufacturer's specifications. The illustrations below show some of the many options available in recessed ceiling fixtures.

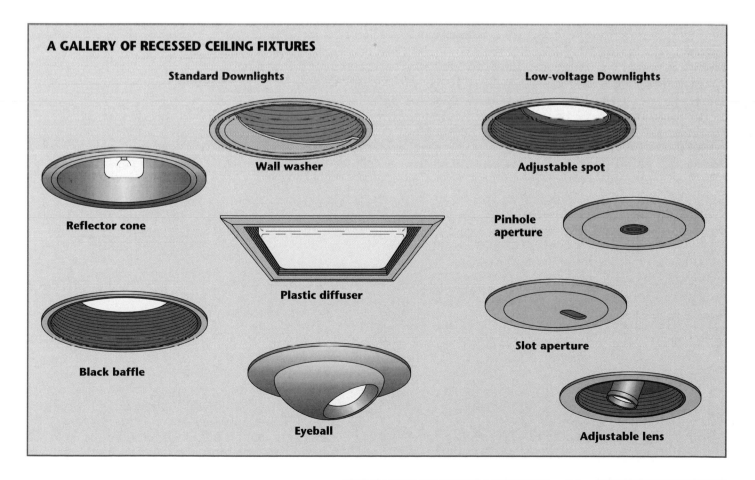

A GALLERY OF RECESSED CEILING FIXTURES

Standard Downlights

Low-voltage Downlights

Wall washer

Adjustable spot

Reflector cone

Pinhole aperture

Plastic diffuser

Slot aperture

Black baffle

Eyeball

Adjustable lens

SURFACE-MOUNTED FIXTURES

Installed either on walls or on ceilings, surface-mounted fixtures are integral to most home lighting designs. Replacing an existing surface-mounted fixture is usually not too difficult. Of course, installing one where there has never been one before will require more wiring work. See page 96 for more on installing fixtures.

Ceiling and wall fixtures: General illumination in traffic areas such as landings, entries, and hallways, is often provided by ceiling or wall fixtures. Kitchens, bathrooms, and workshops benefit from the added light of ceiling fixtures used in conjunction with task lighting on work surfaces.

Fixtures in this category range from functional frosted-glass globes to delicate, candlelike sconces. When selecting a fixture, look closely at the amount of light that bounces off the wall or ceiling to be sure the light will be directed where you want it.

Wall sconces are great for hallways and indirect lighting along walls. Place sconces about 5 1/2 feet from the floor; keep them away from corners—otherwise, they'll create hot spots.

Some building codes require that new kitchens and bathrooms must be outfitted with fluorescent fixtures; check with local building officials or your utility company for details.

Chandeliers and pendant fixtures: For sparkle and style in high-ceilinged entries and above dining and game tables, nothing beats chandeliers and pendant fixtures. These decorative units can provide direct or diffused light—or a combination of the two—for different purposes.

The proportion of the fixture in relation to its surroundings is critical. If the fixture is used over a table, its width should be at least 12 inches less than the width of the table to prevent collisions with diners or passersby. Hanging it about 30 inches above the table surface helps avoid glare. In an entry, be sure to allow enough room below the chandelier to guarantee safe passage for tall people.

Mini-lights and strip lights: Partly for fun, and partly for effective task lighting, mini-lights and strip lights add a splash of light and color to display niches, kitchen counters, stair railings, bathroom mirrors, and just about anywhere else.

A VARIETY OF SURFACE-MOUNTED FIXTURES

Ceiling fan/light

Wall sconce

Ceiling fixture

Fluorescent bar fixture

Pendant fixture

TRACK LIGHTING

A variation on surface-mounted fixtures, track lighting offers great versatility and ease of installation. Tracks are really extended electrical lines, either plugged into an existing receptacle or wired in to a circuit. Fixtures can be mounted anywhere along a line.

A track can be flush-mounted or suspended, and used on ceilings or walls. The plug-in type usually does not require any extra wiring. Track fixtures should generally be fairly close to the wall they're meant to light—within 2 to 4 feet is good. For safety, avoid track lighting in wet areas, such as bathrooms.

Tracks come in a variety of lengths, in single- and multicircuit varieties; the multicircuit type allows for the independent operation of two or more sets of lights. Track connectors allow some systems to be extended indefinitely—in a straight line, at an angle, or even in a rectangular pattern.

Tracks can accommodate pendant fixtures, clip-on lamps, and low-voltage spotlights, as well as a large selection of standard-style fixtures. Like their recessed light counterparts, some low-voltage track fixtures have an integral transformer, while others fit a standard track with an adapter transformer. Another option is to use an external transformer mounted away from the track, which can serve several tracks and lights.

Framing projectors and mini-tracks—scaled-down systems for bookshelves—are especially effective for spotlighting artwork on a wall or shelf.

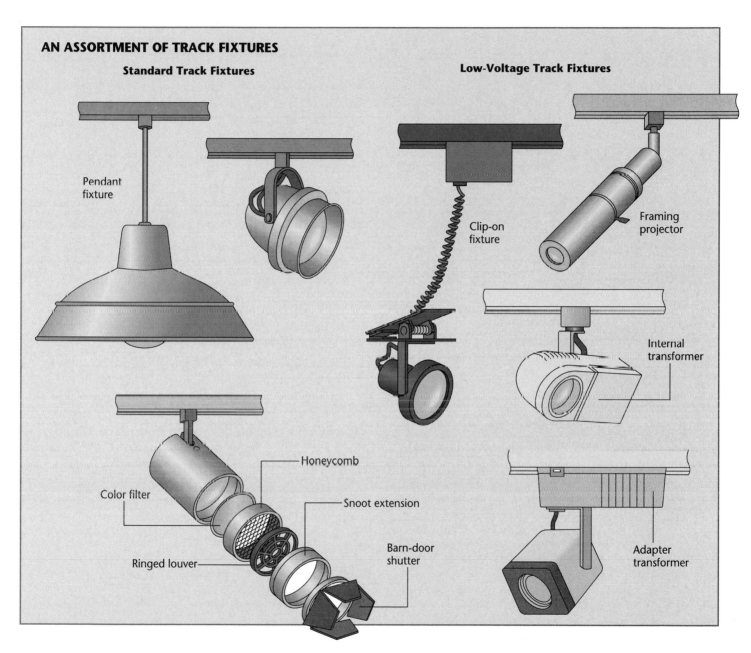

AN ASSORTMENT OF TRACK FIXTURES

Standard Track Fixtures

Low-Voltage Track Fixtures

Pendant fixture

Clip-on fixture

Framing projector

Internal transformer

Color filter

Honeycomb

Snoot extension

Ringed louver

Barn-door shutter

Adapter transformer

ACCESSORIES

Part of what makes a lighting system functional is the ability to direct light where you want it. For this reason, a number of accessories that allow you greater light control are available for different fixtures. Filters, baffles, and louvers can be attached to track lights, recessed downlights, and architectural fixtures to diffuse the light, direct it at various angles, and keep glare out of people's eyes. A number of these accessories are illustrated above for track lighting, but similar accessories exist for other types of lighting, including indirect lighting systems, recessed fixtures, and even surface-mounted fixtures. In general, fixtures with deeply inset bulbs are less likely to produce harsh glare, thus less likely to need accessories.

MOVABLE LIGHT FIXTURES

Table lamps, floor lamps, and small specialty lamps are perhaps the simplest solution to lighting needs. Easy to buy, change, and take along when you move, fixtures within this category can provide any kind of light.

Table lamps: With choices ranging from traditional to avant-garde, you can express your individual taste and style with table lamps. Variety, mobility, and ease of installation add to their appeal.

The choice of a lampshade can be crucial to the table lamp's effectiveness. For example, a difference of only 2 inches in the diameter of the shade's lower edge can make a significant difference in the lamp's spread of light. The bulb's height within the shade also affects illumination: light spreads farther when the bulb is set low in the shade. You can buy extension screws that fit on the lamp harp to adjust shade height.

Floor lamps: The traditional floor lamp is available in many heights; it can serve as either a reading light or a source of soft ambient light. Unobtrusive pharmacy lamps come in various sizes, too, for various tasks such as reading and sewing. Three-source lamps and other lamps with adjustable directional fixtures are good for task lighting.

Bright torcheres, available in both halogen and incandescent versions, bounce light onto the ceiling for a dramatic form of indirect lighting. However, the standard 8-foot ceiling may be too low for the typical 6- to 6½-foot-high torchere—look for a lamp with a built-in diffuser to avoid a hot spot. Some torcheres include a dimmer unit for controlling the light output.

Specialty lamps: Available in new varieties all the time, specialty lamps, such as the traditional picture light or drafting table lamp, fill a specific need yet remain movable, and require no special wiring.

Easily adjusted clip-on lights provide task lighting over beds, desks, and shelves. Uplights can highlight indoor plants or wash walls with light for instant decorating touches. Mini-reflector spotlights are handy for pinpointing paintings or sculptures from a nearby mantelpiece or shelf.

Adjustable task lamps supply a small, bright pool of light while leaving the work area uncluttered. Halogen lamps produce a clean, tight beam. Fluorescent models are great for reducing glare and shadows and are generally more energy efficient than incandescents.

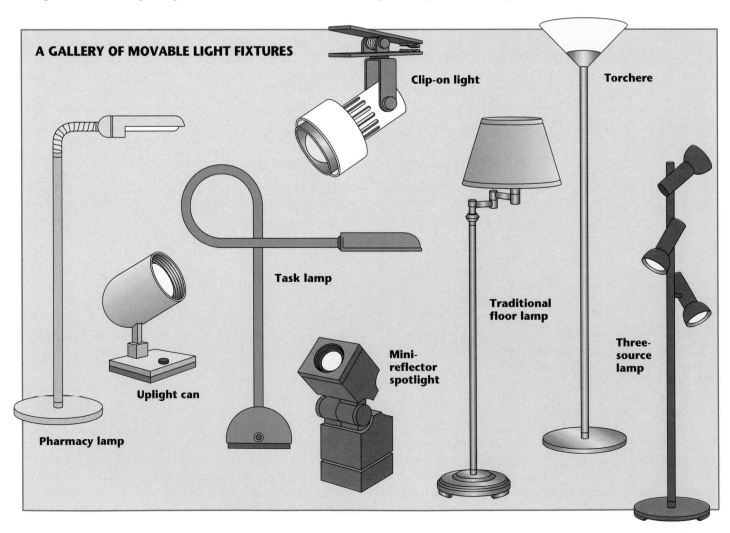

A GALLERY OF MOVABLE LIGHT FIXTURES

Clip-on light

Torchere

Task lamp

Traditional floor lamp

Uplight can

Mini-reflector spotlight

Three-source lamp

Pharmacy lamp

LIGHT BULBS AND TUBES

These simple units work in conjunction with light fixtures (*page 13*) to provide the various types of lighting required in a room or area. Bulbs and tubes can be grouped in general categories according to the way they produce light. The chart on the following pages includes information on a number of different types of bulbs and tubes, including a range of available wattages, typical light outputs, efficacy ratings, and color rendering information, to help you choose the right light source for your situation. Of course, this is only a selection of the available options; visit a lighting showroom or home center for more.

Incandescent bulbs: A tungsten filament burning inside a glass bulb filled with inert gas, usually argon, produces the warm incandescent light that we're all familiar with. Incandescent bulbs have excellent color rendering properties, with CRIs between 95 and 100, but, in general, they're not very efficacious. Use a less costly source (such as fluorescent light) when the warmth and excellent color rendering properties of incandescent light are not crucial.

The most common incandescent bulb is the familiar pear-shaped A-bulb. It comes in different sizes, specified by a number representing the bulb's diameter in eighths of an inch. An A19 bulb, for example, is an A-bulb with a diameter of 19 eighths of an inch, or 2³/₈ inches. Other common bulb shapes are tubular, flame-shaped, and globe-shaped. Three-way bulbs, reduced-wattage bulbs, and long-life bulbs are also available.

For a directional light beam, choose reflector bulbs. Common types are R (reflector) and ER (ellipsoidal reflector), although other shapes are available. PAR (parabolic aluminized reflector) bulbs, once popular for residential outdoor lighting, are being phased out by new energy-efficiency regulations; choose halogen PARs instead. All come in a range of beam spreads, so you can choose the most appropriate one.

Low-voltage incandescent light bulbs are usually small and tend to have a narrow beam spread, making them especially useful in accent lighting, where light must be localized or precisely directed onto a small area. Low-voltage mini-lights are decorative in their own right.

Low-voltage fixtures are relatively expensive to buy, but in general, low-voltage lighting can be energy-efficient if carefully planned.

Halogen bulbs: Longer lasting than their common incandescent counterparts because of chemicals (halogens) included inside the bulb, halogen bulbs are available in a variety of shapes and sizes. Many halogen fixtures use tube-shaped halogen bulbs, but there are a variety of other shapes on the market, including A-bulbs that can replace common incandescent A-bulbs, and various reflectors. Low-voltage halogen bulbs are also available, both for indoor and outdoor use.

Halogen bulbs produce a somewhat whiter light than common incandescents, with good color rendering properties. Be careful not to touch halogen bulbs, because they can get very hot. Most bulbs require fixtures designed specifically for halogen bulbs. Shop carefully: some fixtures on the market are not approved by the Underwriters' Laboratories (UL).

Fluorescent tubes: When electricity passes through a fluorescent tube, it burns the mercury vapor there, producing ultraviolet light, which is reradiated as visible light by the phosphors coating the inside of the tube. The type of phosphors used determines the color of the light as well as its color rendering properties. Triphosphors, also called rare earth phosphors, are best. They're more expensive than tubes with other coatings (called halophosphors), but they're also more efficacious.

Fluorescent tubes are available either straight in various diameters (1-inch T8 and 1¹/₂-inch T12 tubes are most common) or bent into a variety of shapes, such as circline or U-shaped. You can also get compact fluorescents and screwbase fluorescents that screw into a socket, which can be used to replace incandescent bulbs.

Tubes require a ballast to ignite and maintain the electrical flow. Electronic ballasts, although more expensive than magnetic ballasts, are more energy-efficient and quieter. (The noise typical of older fluorescent fixtures is actually caused by the magnetic ballast not by the tubes themselves.) The ballast may be integral to the tube or separate. Separate ballasts can sometimes be used for more than one tube. Separate ballasts often lead to savings in the long run, because the tubes tend to wear out before the ballasts do. If you buy tubes with integral ballasts, you'll be paying for a new ballast every time you replace a tube; with separate ballasts, you can replace only the tubes as needed.

High-intensity-discharge (HID) bulbs: Various types of bulbs (mercury vapor, metal halide, and high-pressure sodium) are grouped in this category. All produce light when electricity excites specific gases inside the bulb. Metal halide and high-pressure sodium bulbs are both very efficacious, much more so than mercury vapor bulbs. These lights are often used outdoors because they produce a lot of light with low energy input and are very long lasting. None of them have exceptional color rendering properties. Improved-color versions are available for use when good color rendering properties are especially important, but they are not as energy efficient as the standard types. Visit a lighting showroom or consult a professional for information on the type most appropriate for your situation.

LIGHT BULB AND TUBE TYPES

		Description	Light Output (lumens)
INCANDESCENT			
A-bulb		Familiar pear shape; frosted or clear.	460 to 2,220
Three-way		A-bulb shape; frosted; two filaments provide three light levels.	300 to 2,140
Reduced-wattage long-life		A-bulb shape; frosted; lasts longer but produces less light.	700 to 2,145
G-Globe		Ball-shaped bulb, 2" to 6" in diameter; frosted or clear.	245 to 740
T-Tubular		Tube-shaped, from 5" long; frosted or clear.	580 to 2,220
Flame-shaped (Candle)		Decorative; specially coated.	325 to 650
R-Reflector		White or silver coating directs light out end of funnel-shaped bulb.	410 to 1,900 (N/A for heat lamps)
ER-Ellipsoidal reflector		Shape and coating focus light 2" ahead of bulb, then light spreads out.	850
Silvered bowl		Same shape as A-bulb; silvered cap cuts glare, produces indirect light.	760
Low-voltage reflector spot		Similar to standard R-bulb; directs light in various beam spreads and distances.	400
Low-voltage mini-lights		Like Christmas tree lights, encased in flexible, waterproof plastic.	Decorative product; minimal light output.
HALOGEN			
Tube-shaped		Tube-shaped; nondirectional; protected by glass cover due to high temperatures.	5,600 to 11,100
PAR flood		Wide "flood" beam spread; good beam control; efficacious.	540 to 1,270
Low-voltage MR-16 (multifaceted reflector)		Tiny projector bulb with 2" diameter; gives small circle of light from a distance.	280 to 960
FLUORESCENT			
Linear tube		Tube-shaped, 5" to 96" long; needs special fixture and ballast.	390 to 3,800
U-shaped tube		U-shaped with base; typically 5$1/4$" to 7$1/2$" long.	2,400 to 2,800
Circline		Circular, 6" to 16" long; may replace A-bulbs or require special fixtures.	250 to 2,100
Compact screwbase		Variety of sizes and color temperatures; can replace A-bulbs.	450 to 1,550
HIGH-INTENSITY-DISCHARGE (HID)			
Metal halide		Almost twice as efficacious as old mercury vapor; needs special ballast and fixture.	5,000 to 10,000
High-pressure sodium		Yellow-hued light; needs special ballast and fixture.	2,250 to 9,500

Common Wattages	Efficacy (lumens per watt)	CCT (K)	CRI	Bulb Life (hours)
25 to 150	14.5 to 18.5	2,800	95+	750 to 2,500
30/70/100 to 50/100/150	10 to 15	2,800	95+	1,000 to 1,600
52 to 135	13.5 to 16	2,800	95+	2,500
40 to 60	6 to 12	2,800	95+	1,500 to 2,500
50 to 150	7.5 to 10	2,800	95+	1,200 to 1,500
40 to 60	8 to 11	2,800	95+	1,500
50 to 250	8 to 12.5 .	2,800	95+	2,000 to 5,000
75	11.5	2,800	95+	2,000
60	12.5	2,700 to 3,000	95+	1,000
50	8	3,050	95+	4,000
0.84	N/A	N/A	95+	22 years (estimated)
300 to 500	19 to 23	3,050	95+	2,000
25 to 90	11 to 15	3,050	95+	2,000 to 2,500
20 to 50	14 to 19	2,925 to 3,050	95+	2,000 to 4,000
8 to 110	35 to 48	3,000 to 4,200	52 to 80+	7,500 to 24,000
31 to 40	70 to 78	3,000 to 4,200	62 to 80+	12,000 to 20,000
5 to 32	50 to 66	2,700 to 4,200	52 to 82+	12,000
11 to 27	41 to 58	2,700 to 2,800	81 to 84	9,000 to 10,000
70 to 100	71 to 100	3,700 to 4,000	65 to 70	7,500 to 20,000
35 to 100	64 to 95	2,100	22	16,000 to 24,000

OUTDOOR LIGHTING

Plan your home's outdoor lighting—12-volt systems, 120-volt systems, or a combination—much as you would its indoor counterpart. It's easiest to begin by pinpointing areas which will require night lighting and the ways in which these spots can be best lighted.

There are various reasons for illuminating the yard and house exterior, including facilitating outdoor activity, illuminating the landscape, and keeping people safe and property secure. Well-planned outdoor lighting integrates safety and security lighting within an esthetically pleasing lighting design.

Over the following pages, we'll explore the world of outdoor lighting, from the fixtures involved, to the techniques commonly used.

ELIMINATING GLARE

Regardless of the lighting chosen, avoiding glare from light fixtures is a prime concern. Glare is responsible for the discomfort we feel when looking at a light that's too bright or one that's aimed directly into our sight line. At night, because the contrast between the dark and a light source is so great, glare can be a persistent problem. Several methods of minimizing glare are discussed here. As well, refer to the section on avoiding glare indoors, on page 8.

Placing and directing fixtures: The best way to avoid glare is to place fixtures out of sight lines, either very low or very high, along a walk, or up in a tree, for example. Then, direct the fixtures so that only the effect of the light is noticed. Avoid bright spots of light.

Multiple sources of light mean guests can approach this entrance without being confronted by glare. The glass-covered arch, the focus of the lighting design, is washed by downlights next to the beams. Unobtrusive strip lights indicate the edges of the low triangular steps, and uplights accent trees and shrubs around the lawn without producing uncomfortably bright spots of light.
ARCHITECT: BRIAN SHORE

Using more fixtures: Rather than using one high-wattage light outside the front door, it's at once less glaring and more inviting to use several lower-wattage lights strategically placed in the yard. A little light goes a long way at night.

Using shielded fixtures: In a shielded fixture, the bulb area is completely hidden by an opaque covering that directs the light away from a viewer's eyes. The eye instead sees the warm glow of a lighted object rather than a concentrated hot spot of light.

OUTDOOR LIGHTING SYSTEMS

Low-voltage lighting systems *(page 13)* are frequently used outdoors. They're safer to use and install, require less energy to run, and can be installed with less hassle than standard-current—120-volt—systems.

Installing a low-voltage system is fairly simple. Cable can usually lie on top of the ground—but keep it out of the way by covering it with mulch or running it along the edge of a pathway or deck. As well, most fixtures connect easily to cables and no grounding hookups are required. You won't need any permits to install a system that extends from a plug-in transformer—the most common kind. See page 106 for more information.

In addition to the packaged low-voltage systems available, you can use low-voltage PAR spotlights to light trees or larger areas. Halogen MR-16s are increasingly popular for outdoor accent lighting.

Although somewhat more difficult to install, the standard 120-volt system has some advantages outdoors: Lights with a wider beam spread can be used, allowing a single fixture to light a greater area, and highly efficacious, long-lasting high-intensity-discharge (HID) bulbs can be used. As well, power tools and patio heaters can be plugged into 120-volt outdoor outlets.

Whatever system you use, aim for controlled lighting. Excessive light that spills over onto neighboring properties not only frustrates other residents, it wastes energy. Good outdoor lighting schemes suit the lighting—both fixtures and bulbs—to the need.

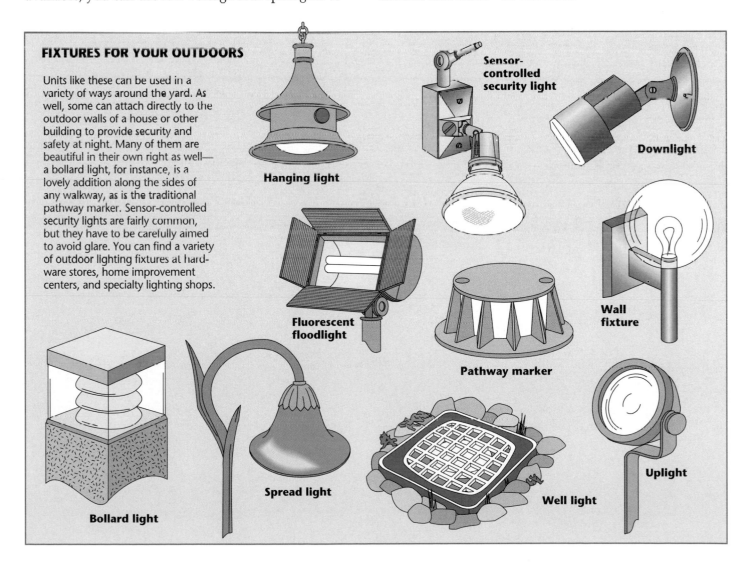

FIXTURES FOR YOUR OUTDOORS

Units like these can be used in a variety of ways around the yard. As well, some can attach directly to the outdoor walls of a house or other building to provide security and safety at night. Many of them are beautiful in their own right as well—a bollard light, for instance, is a lovely addition along the sides of any walkway, as is the traditional pathway marker. Sensor-controlled security lights are fairly common, but they have to be carefully aimed to avoid glare. You can find a variety of outdoor lighting fixtures at hardware stores, home improvement centers, and specialty lighting shops.

Hanging light

Sensor-controlled security light

Downlight

Fluorescent floodlight

Pathway marker

Wall fixture

Bollard light

Spread light

Well light

Uplight

LIGHTING FOR SAFETY AND DECORATION

Around your property you'll have several areas that require lighting. You'll need lighting around the front entrance, but you'll also want to consider other areas, such as decks and patios or pools and spas. Ideally, outdoor lighting should combine style and safety.

Front door: The front door should be lit as the focal point of your design, a welcoming light to draw people from both the driveway and the street. Light should be bright enough to see a caller's face and the house numbers should be clearly visible. Choose fixtures with frosted or translucent stained glass or make sure they're shielded to avoid uncomfortably bright light and glare.

Front walks and steps: The front walkway should be only softly lit, so it doesn't detract from the focus on the front door. Low fixtures that spread soft pools of light can greet guests and highlight your garden's virtues along the walk. If the house has deep eaves or an overhang extending the walk's length, weatherproof downlights will illuminate the walk and plantings with no visible fixtures.

Steps will usually be adequately lighted by fixtures at the front door. Steps set some distance away from the front door, even if only single steps, may require their own light. Try mounting a small fixture above the steps, or building in a light under the stairs or along a wall or railing.

Driveways and garages: Especially if they're long and wooded, driveways should have some kind of light to

Spread lighting
Light up your shrubbery with spread lights placed in the planting beds themselves. Try different colored bulbs for different effects.

Path lighting
Low or slightly raised fixtures that spread soft pools of light can define a walkway and highlight elements of the garden.

Downlighting
Use this technique to gently light up porches, patios, and walkways. It's also good for accenting trees, flowers, and shrubs, while providing enough light at night to maneuver.

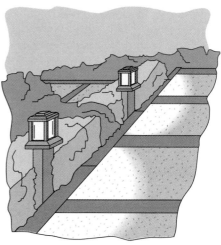

Diffused lighting
A low level of lighting is often enough for low-traffic areas. Light railings and fences indirectly from underneath or behind to outline the edges of the structures.

Moonlighting
Used to approximate the normal effect of moonlight, uplights and downlights placed within the foliage of a tree will provide enough light to distinguish the tree from the rest of the lawn, but not enough to call harsh attention to itself.

define their boundaries. Downlights positioned in the trees are effective and out of drivers' sight lines. Fixtures at ground level should be carefully positioned and shielded to prevent glare in a driver's eyes.

The garage area needs security lighting, ideally controlled by switches inside and out. Motion-sensitive lights, which turn off when no motion occurs within a preset time, may be a good choice. But keep in mind that the movements of animals may trigger the light.

Other house approaches: Adequate lighting at the back gate and other house approaches offers a measure of security. It's best to install individual light fixtures where they're needed, rather than attempting to light all areas of the property with fixtures attached to the house; house walls are not high enough to project light very far without causing uncomfortable glare.

Motion detectors are a good choice here, too, to turn these lights on and off as needed.

Decks and patios: Dim lighting is often enough for quiet conversation or alfresco dining, so consider subtle, low-voltage lighting for these areas. Lighting steps, railings, or benches indirectly from underneath, or directly with strings of mini-lights, allows you to outline the edges of structures for safety, too.

Stronger lights are usually needed for serving or barbecuing areas. Downlights are a popular choice, but indirect lighting diffused through plastic or another translucent material is also useful.

Swimming pools and spas: Light these areas for safety, but don't forget that they should be attractive from inside the house.

Many pools have underwater lights. To avoid glare, especially if the light is in view of the house or patio sitting area, use a dimmer. For relaxing and entertaining, a soft glow which outlines the pool edges will do. Use the light at maximum brightness when children are swimming. Low spotlights muffled by foliage or trained on walls can provide dramatic indirect lighting, reflecting on the pool surface when the pool lights are off.

Popular for an evening soak, a spa or hot tub can be illuminated with low-voltage twinkling mini-lights that will subtly outline its perimeter or steps.

Foliage: Uplighting, downlighting, and spread lighting are all common techniques for illuminating foliage, combining functional and decorative lighting.

For a dappled, "moonlight" effect, place both uplights and downlights in a large tree to highlight some of the foliage and create shadows on the ground below. To silhouette a tree or shrub, aim a spotlight or wall washer at a fence or wall from close behind the plant. Decorative mini-lights help outline trees and lend sparkle to the garden.

Use uplights, downlights, and accent lighting on separate switches to create any number of interesting garden effects. As well, dimmers can be used for even more lighting flexibility.

A classical poolside loggia is ready for a quiet summer evening's repose (left). The dining table features a hanging candelabra with votive candles producing a soft glow; it's augmented with a central downlight above. Accent light comes from 75-watt reflector bulbs housed in arbor-mounted downlights; two flank the back of each column and backlight them dramatically. The glowing water is lit by two wall-mounted underwater fixtures.
LANDSCAPE ARCHITECT: ROBERT W. CHITTOCK

ROOM-BY-ROOM LIGHTING OPTIONS

With a sound understanding of how lighting affects a room's style, decorating your home with light can be an exciting, creative process. Whether replacing fixtures, working with new rooms, or simply adding a delicate accent to an already beautiful space, working lighting into the design will offer brilliant results.

In this chapter we'll show you how the proper use of lighting techniques can add charm and dazzling effects to every part of your home and property. Areas as diverse as hallways and entrances *(opposite)*, kitchens *(page 44)*, home offices *(page 53)*, and stairways *(page 56)* can all benefit from a touch of well-directed light. Proper lighting is equally important in bedrooms *(page 58)* and bathrooms *(page 64)*, as well as in areas where you'll be entertaining guests, such as living areas *(page 30)* and dining rooms *(page 38)*. Don't forget outdoor areas *(page 69)*—light works wonders around paths and walkways, and in the backyard.

The photos on the following pages are examples of how the elusive quality of light can be captured and harnessed in your home and outdoor surroundings. The other chapters in this book will give you concrete help with achieving results similar to these.

Welcome guests with a gentle downlight over the door, a leaded-glass window lit from inside, and a lidded wall washer in the alcove. The downlight by the door is diffuse enough so there's no uncomfortable glare, yet strong enough to light the doorstep.
LIGHTING DESIGN: DONALD MAXCY
ARCHITECT: KIP STEWART

HALLWAYS AND ENTRANCES

Hallways and entrances serve many functions in the home, from leading guests in from the front door to directing traffic between rooms. As the first area of your home that guests will see, entrances should be warmly lighted. As routes for human traffic, hallways should be neither much dimmer nor much brighter than adjoining rooms so that your eyes don't have to make radical adjustments when you're moving from room to room.

When planning hall lighting, remember to keep it simple and safe. Wall or ceiling fixtures can be placed to guide guests into the traffic pattern. As with stairways *(page 56)*, it's helpful to plan three-way switches at both ends. A dimmer can replace one switch for controlled decorative effects.

A hallway can be an exciting art gallery *(page 29)*, but be sure the light is dimmable, or consider a second set of soft fixtures or night lights for late-night hallway safety.

On these pages, you'll find examples of how the different lighting techniques discussed in the first chapter can be put to good use in your home's hallways.

A faux "skylight" effect from hidden halogen lights adds sunlike brightness to this hallway (right). In the background, an aimable downlight accents the wall-hung painting.
LIGHTING DESIGN: LINDA FERRY
ARCHITECT: LEE VON HASSELN

Low-voltage track fixtures and attractive displays draw visitors into this hallway gallery (right). Two MR-16 very-narrow spot fixtures are trained on the vase and credenza; floods and more spots alternate down the hallway. Power comes to each fixture through a mono-point—a short length of track.
LIGHTING DESIGN: EPIFANIO JUAREZ (JUAREZ DESIGN)

The curved central hallway (opposite) of a rebuilt townhouse was the perfect place to show off an art collection, but lighting a nonlinear space with changing needs in mind required something new in tracks: a curved, custom statement. The elegant pewter track blends well with the softly fauxed walls, while the "lily" shades, each with its own MR-16 very-narrow spot, highlight rows of framed prints.
LIGHTING DESIGN: TERRY OHM
INTERIOR DESIGN:
ANN MAURICE INTERIOR DESIGN

Sun-filled by day, this hallway (left) is lighted for a soft nighttime look. Pairs of wall fixtures illuminate the floor and steps, and send a glow of light upward. A pinhole-aperture spotlight high on the wall highlights the trailing plant. Two custom-made kite lanterns sway gracefully as they fill the hall with light.
LIGHTING DESIGN: RICHARD PETERS
LANTERN DESIGN: CHARLES MOORE
AND CHRISTINA BEEBE
ARCHITECT: CHARLES MOORE

LIVING AREAS

Providing light for an active family's needs in living rooms and family rooms can be a challenge. You'll want to include well-shielded task lighting for such activities as reading and playing games, as well as accent lighting on artwork or architectural features. Low levels of ambient light set a congenial mood for entertaining or watching television. The different types of lighting are discussed more fully on page 5.

The trick to good living area lighting is to provide a variety of sources so you can have the greatest flexibility in light levels. Built-in architectural fixtures, such as valances, soffits, and coves, are effective ambient sources. Traditional floor and table lamps are enjoying a renaissance, with many new design options on the market.

Such fixtures are often chosen for their esthetic appeal, but practical considerations, such as proper shading to avoid glare, should also influence your decision.

Dimmers, scene panels, or computer controls allow you to adjust multiple sources for a variety of uses and moods—from functional to romantic or dramatic. Three-way bulbs provide added flexibility—you can choose the highest level for visually difficult tasks and a lower level for ambient light.

In this section, we'll explore light in a home's living and entertaining areas. Keep in mind that rooms hosting multiple activities, as most living areas do, require multiple lighting sources and that fixture types, styles, and light levels should harmonize from space to space.

This family room (left), decorated with a Latin-inspired flair, is filled with ambient daylight from open windows. Downlights accent artwork on the window wall and on the mantle above the fireplace.

Collectibles are pinpointed using track fixtures (PAR-36 with narrow and very-narrow spot spreads) installed in beams high overhead (below). These lights are even powerful enough to pass through a thick glass coffee table. Soft, indirect fill light comes from 15-watt incandescents tucked into the clerestory space overhead. Decorative wall sconces both inside and out, visible beyond the glass exterior wall, tie indoor and outdoor lighting together.

ARCHITECTS: BUFF, SMITH & HENSMAN
DESIGN: BOB MOORE

Two people can relax and read in this comfortable room. Task lighting from lamps on either side of the couch allows for a pleasant afternoon's read without eyestrain.

A decorative standing lamp with glass housing washes the wall and nearby areas with light (left). Aimable downlights accent the art display and items on the coffee table, while recessed downlights (not shown) bring light to the sitting area. The contents of the wall cabinet's glass display shelves are highlighted by downlights inside— these can also provide a soothing light level when used alone.

Low in voltage, but high in drama, this vaulted great room (right) is tied together by computer-controlled, multilayer lighting options. The two-story living room space is bridged by an MR-16 cable system running in two directions. Fixtures fitted with wall washers and slot apertures light the decorative screen and prints, respectively; the glass shelf alcove is accented from above by a built-in PAR lamp. Finally, decorative strip lights run out of sight behind the floor overhang and around the built-in table. There are control panels in several spots, and all fixtures are dimmer-controlled.
Architect: Peter B. Harmon, AIA
Design: Peter Dempsey

With aimable downlights directed at the painting behind the couch, the glass coffee table, the mirror-backed display counter, and the art above the fireplace, this room has plenty of accent light. Recessed downlights and daylight from the window provide fill light. The spread of illumination is maximized by the light-colored walls and couch.
LIGHTING DESIGN: RANDALL WHITEHEAD (LIGHT SOURCE)
INTERIOR DESIGN: LAWRENCE MASNADA

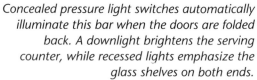

Concealed pressure light switches automatically illuminate this bar when the doors are folded back. A downlight brightens the serving counter, while recessed lights emphasize the glass shelves on both ends.
INTERIOR DESIGNER: CAROLYN FIELDER (CAMPBELL DESIGN ASSOCIATES)

The ceiling-hung pendant fixture (above), with its checkerboard patterned glass, brings plenty of diffused light to this room's pool table. The cue ball, patterned to match the shade, brings a touch of whimsy to the game.
LIGHTING DESIGN: RANDALL WHITEHEAD (LIGHT SOURCE) PENDANT FIXTURE DESIGN AND FABRICATION: PAM MORRIS (EXCITING LIGHTING) INTERIOR DESIGN: BARBARA JACOBS INTERIOR DESIGN AND JANICE NAYMARK INTERIOR DESIGN

Two torcheres wash gentle light onto textured green wallpaper and a cream-colored ceiling, offering flexibility in light levels and maintaining visual symmetry in the drawing room at left. Daylight's potential for harsh glare is beautifully controlled with colored wood shutters on the large picture window. Daylight sources on either side of the room (not shown) provide yet more fill light. Oriental boxes and other delicate artifacts add to the room's Eastern-inspired elegance.

This richly colored room (above) is lighted by a square perimeter of recessed downlights along the ceiling beams. Ample reading light is provided by several table and floor lamps throughout the space. During daylight hours, the drapes across the tall French doors can be kept open to let in plenty of light.

Contemporary design is uncluttered by visible fixtures in this open living room (opposite). Ambient light, which washes walls and grazes decorative columns, comes from track fixtures concealed in the skylight well. Light spread is maximized by white walls and light-colored furniture. Discreet downlights add directional task light and accent light in the sitting area.

ARCHITECT: JAMES GILLAM ARCHITECTS
DESIGN: JANE NISSEN LAIDLEY

DINING ROOMS

Elegant or informal, your dining area will benefit from careful lighting. Sparkling light from a chandelier, a pendant fixture, or downlights, combined with soft, indirect light on the walls, and perhaps candles on the table, will help put your guests in a relaxed mood.

The main focus of dining room lighting should be the dining table itself—whether it's a small, circular table for intimate dinners or a long, rectangular buffet table for a larger gathering. But it's best if a decorative fixture like a chandelier is not the only light source—it's likely to cause discomfort when turned up high.

Augment the light over the table with a separate set of fixtures, perhaps over the buffet, to supply light for serving as well as background light at mealtimes.

Dimmers can be a real plus—turned up high, the light aids in the task of setting the table or directing guests; on low, the gentle beam creates a festive atmosphere and minimizes glare.

This section offers a guided tour of some beautifully lit dining rooms. Whether your dining area is mainly used for family mealtimes or is the main entertaining center in your home, you'll find creative inspiration here.

Three beaded pendants hang from low-voltage cables by weighted counter-balances, marking the line of a sturdy waxed-pine dining table (right). Fixed table lamps are mounted in window alcoves flanking the far fireplace; MR-16 monospots wash fir-paneled walls, providing ambient fill light in the middle zones. Display cabinets are backlit from within with strip lights tucked behind rear valances.
ARCHITECT: BACKEN, ARRAGONI & ROSS

Recessed downlights over a built-in buffet not only supply light for serving, but also highlight a special piece of art. Sconces wash the walls with soft pools of light.
ARCHITECT: STEPHEN MUSE
INTERIOR DESIGNER: DENNIS CANNADAY

A candelabra hanging lamp such as the one at right adds a definitively elegant flair to any dining area. Candle incandescent bulbs set in holders bring delicate light to mealtime without any uncomfortable glare. Recessed MR-16 downlights between ceiling beams provide ambient light, and windows give the room an open-air feeling.
ARCHITECTS: BACKEN, ARRAGONI & ROSS

In this corner dining area, picture lights accent artwork and set an intimate mood. An invasive hanging fixture was replaced with an inconspicuous recessed downlight to visually enlarge the small space.
INTERIOR DESIGNER: CHER STONE BEALL
(CASHMERE & COMPANY)

A clever alternative to the standard dining-room chandelier, this hanging fixture (right) combines sandblasted woodworking clamps and thick plate glass to form a transparent shelf for votive candles. An MR-16 downlight shines through the center, providing extra punch. The clamps are anchored to the ceiling with pipe flanges. An aluminum chair rail houses additional candles; their light is reflected off more plate glass that's floated in front of the dining room wall.
DESIGN: BRIAN A. MURPHY AND FRO VAKILI
(BAM CONSTRUCTION/DESIGN)

Custom wall sconces in a self-contained breakfast area (left) provide ambient light and decorative flair. The central mirror helps amplify daylight and echoes the view of a nearby garden.
INTERIOR DESIGN:
OSBURN DESIGN

A greenhouse addition can lend an airy, outdoor feel to a cramped interior (opposite), but how can you subtly add enough light at night—or, occasionally, to fill in during high-contrast daylight hours? This designer chose low-voltage cable lights—thin wire supports and decorative shades float unobtrusively while adding a touch of fun.
INTERIOR DESIGN: OSBURN DESIGN

Unless there's outside light, the view disappears at night. This dining alcove (left) gets cheery daylight through ganged double-hung window units by day; at night, the sill-mounted outdoor planter boxes are spotlighted by down-lights anchored to the eaves overhead. Inside, a floor lamp with a delicate shade provides soft light.
ARCHITECTS: BACKEN, ARRAGONI & ROSS

A three-tiered paper shade makes a handsome dining room accent (right). The translucent shade turns direct potential glare from a hanging pendant fixture to a soft sidewise glow while shooting direct light toward the ceiling, where it's converted to a broader, softer bounce source. Staggered wall sconces following the angle of the stairs add fill light.
ARCHITECT:
JAMES GILLAM ARCHITECTS
DESIGN:
JANE NISSEN LAIDLEY

KITCHENS

Often a social gathering place, the kitchen benefits from general lighting for after-hours snacks or entertaining. And whether there is one cook hard at work on a culinary masterpiece, or a whole crew of young kitchen helpers, task lighting for the sink, countertops, and rangetop is essential.

You'll want strong, shadowless light right over each kitchen work area. In most cases, shielded strip lights under the cabinets are best to light the counter area, while direct downlights can illuminate the sink and work islands. Light-colored countertops and walls add brightness, because they reflect light. It's best to hide under-cabinet lights behind a trim strip or valance.

If your countertops, stoves, and work spaces are well-lighted, general illumination need only be bright enough to ensure safe movement about the room. Architectural coves (uplights) above the cabinets are a good choice. Multiple sources and dimmer controls allow you to turn up the light to full-throttle when working or down to a warm glow after hours. When choosing fixtures, whether decorative or functional, keep in mind that since they're in the kitchen, they'll need frequent cleaning.

In this section, you'll see how some designers use light to transform the most often-used room of the house into more than just a utilitarian work center. You're sure to find ideas you can duplicate in your own home.

Windows above this kitchen counter (right) provide ample daytime work light; the decorative wall sconce fills in during evening hours.
LIGHTING: KAREN THOMPSON (ARCHETILE) DESIGN: TERRY SANDERS, VIRGINIA SMITH, SHARRY HICKY, AND GEORGANNE THURSTON

A central, lowered "beam," built up from lightly pickled oak, houses recessed halogen downlights and follows the work surfaces of the tile island at left, providing strong lighting where it's most needed. General lighting is provided by track fixtures, not visible in the photo, tucked along some of the beams.
LIGHTING DESIGN: LINDA FERRY
ARCHITECT: CHARLES ROSE
INTERIOR DESIGN: MICHELLE PHEASANT DESIGN

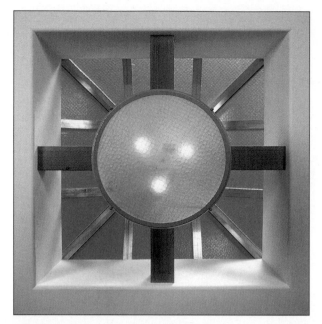

Finding the right fixtures to light this sleek, contemporary kitchen with its soaring 16-foot ceiling was a challenge. Ceiling uplights and incandescent lights under the wall-hung cabinets add warm, soft illumination, while four suspended stainless-steel halogen fixtures direct light onto the island.
ARCHITECT: CHARLES M. MOORE

The U-shaped kitchen, with center breakfast-counter island (below), is lighted by hanging pendant lights and recessed downlights. Day or night, a custom skylight and pendant fixture provide ample ambient light. A closer look at the pendant fixture and skylight is shown at left.
DESIGN: GEOFFREY FROST (KITCHEN STUDIO LOS ANGELES)

In this kitchen, available daylight is maximized by two rows of windows on the north-facing wall. A variety of electric light sources fill in: fluorescent tubes both under and over the cabinets, MR-16 downlights, and 100-watt A-bulbs in decorative Italian glass pendants provide both task and ambient lighting. Incandescent strip lights add a warm glow to the display niche over the refrigerator.

INTERIOR DESIGN AND LIGHTING: MARGARET M. WIMMER
ARCHITECT: CARRASCO & ASSOCIATES

To solve the problem of a hard-to-light dark redwood ceiling, this designer installed strings of stylish low-voltage cable tracks to follow the major traffic corridors, featuring double diffusing "tents" for glare-free ambient light, then added decorative track pendants over the island (above). A standard track is tucked behind the popout window's header beam, lighting the sink area; additional lights above and below the wall cabinets provide extra light in the food preparation area.
LIGHTING DESIGN: RANDALL WHITEHEAD (LIGHT SOURCE)

Pendant lights hanging from coiled wire add a subtle decorative touch in this breakfast area (right). Their incandescent bulbs cast a warm glow over the countertop.
DESIGN: ADELE CRAWFORD
PAINTED FINISHES

The owner of this kitchen—part of an old remodeled winery—wanted lots of light, but the raised ceiling made it a challenging task. Stylish red Italian pendants, each housing tiny but efficient halogen bulbs, solved the problem and defined the space. Electrical conduit, painted white, leads from the roofline down to the fixtures, which were meant to be ceiling mounted. **LIGHTING DESIGN: MELINDA MORRISON LIGHTING DESIGN ARCHITECTS: BYRON KUTH, LIZ RANIERI, AND DOUG THORNLEY (KUTH/RANIERI)**

The main light fixture at right, with its three polished rods suspended from the ceiling on decorative metal anchors, shows that fixtures can be both practical and highly decorative. The recessed bulbs in the center rod are quite inconspicuous but provide good task lighting over the work area. Track spotlights between open ceiling beams, and wall sconces in the background provide the room's fill light.
INTERIOR DESIGN: OSBURN DESIGN

Three light sources make this kitchen bright and cheerful. A contemporary pendant fixture over the kitchen table supplies localized light for dining, supplemented by the natural light that filters through the window coverings. Recessed ceiling fixtures elsewhere in the room fill in with general illumination.

51

This kitchen's angled peninsula is highlighted by open recessed downlights (right), which brighten up the dark cabinets and appliances. Butcher-block countertops and oak flooring add contrast. In the background, a low-voltage downlight showcases Italian collectibles inside the glass wall cabinet.
DESIGN: PLUS KITCHENS

Banks of south-facing windows plus uplights along one wall direct light up and off a high, curved white ceiling (left), providing plenty of ambient light for the kitchen and the rest of this open living space. Fluorescent tubes hidden under the cabinets take care of task lighting for the countertop.
**ARCHITECT:
OLSON/SUNDBERG
ARCHITECTS**

HOME OFFICES

Because more people are working out of the home, there is an increasing need for bright, comfortable home offices. Even if your work space is confined to the corner of a large room, effective lighting techniques will help define the area and make it possible to work without eyestrain or distracting shadows.

When arranging light fixtures and choosing bulbs, make sure that your work surface is free from shadows. With a combination of general lighting and adjustable task lighting, you can avoid strong contrasts between a specific work area and the rest of the room.

If your surroundings have a high reflectance, task areas will be easier to light. For example, a light-colored blotter on the desk and light-hued walls and ceiling above will reflect light directly back onto the work area.

Fluorescent architectural fixtures or built-in downlights work well for ambient lighting in an office. For close work, a compact fluorescent or halogen task lamp is a good choice.

In this section, you'll see how you can use good lighting techniques to improve the overall look and function of your home office.

The lighting in this study was designed to look "soft," in contrast to the hard, industrial concrete and stone. A low-voltage cable system follows the curve of the desk alcove above the floating maple shelves; aluminum louvers control light spill and add style. Task lamps provide adjustable work light. Light grazing the stone wall provides ambient fill; it's created by a string of reflector lamps (smoother than PAR bulbs) hidden inside a light well.
LIGHTING DESIGN: MELINDA MORRISON LIGHTING DESIGN
ARCHITECTS: BYRON KUTH, LIZ RANIERI, AND DOUG THORNLEY (KUTH/RANIERI)

A wall of windows fills this study with warmth and light during the day. Undercabinet fixtures provide task light for the countertop desks, and a brass reading lamp helps even more on the right-side desk. Above, recessed downlights and a fixture hidden in the faux-skylight recess provide additional ambient light when necessary.

ARCHITECTS: JIM OLSON AND MATTHEW STANNARD (OLSON/SUNDBERG ARCHITECTS)

In a home office tucked into a corner of the kitchen, a small built-in desk utilizes the same type of under-cabinet fixtures that light other countertops. There's ample task light thrown to the desk surface, which gets a lot of use as the command center for the household.
ARCHITECT: PAT CROGHAN

A garden view, bright white surfaces, and effective lighting help make this converted basement office into a cheery, productive work space. Glass pendant fixtures follow the L-shaped work counters, and a shiny chrome lamp boosts task lighting at the drafting board.
INTERIOR DESIGN: GAIL WOOLAWAY & ASSOCIATES

STAIRWAYS

Leading guests from floor to floor, stairways are an important part of any multilevel home. With a full staircase—or even just two steps down to another level—it's important to provide adequate light for safety.

The nosing or edge of each tread and the depth of each step should be well-defined. One way to achieve this is to combine a downlight over the stairs to light the edges, with a softer light projected from the landing below to define the depth. Another option is to build low-voltage fixtures into the wall just above every third or fourth step. Lights hidden in a handrail are another unobtrusive yet effective way to light the tops of treads.

As with hallways *(page 27)*, be sure that the fixtures do not direct any blinding glare into people's eyes as they make their way along the stairway. Turn to page 5 for more on the elements of good lighting design.

On these pages, three beautifully lit stairways offer ideas you can apply in your own home.

Glowing mini-lights on a remote transformer light the display niche in the foreground, while an MR-16 fixture on a mono-point illuminates the stairside niche (opposite). Adjustable halogen downlights not visible in the photo wash the walls with light, and tiny aisle lights beside the stair treads keep climbers on course.
DESIGN: EPIFANIO JUAREZ (JUAREZ DESIGN)

Each bold vertical is highlighted by a recessed 12-volt, 20-watt stair fixture (above), aimed to wash out and down for safe treading. A remote transformer feeds the efficient quartz lamps, which can also be dimmed to glow softly like night-lights.
LIGHTING DESIGN: BECCA FOSTER
OWNER: DAVID HILL ASIAN ART

Stairs should be lit for safety, but that doesn't preclude the dramatic. This U-shaped staircase (right) features wall-recessed stair lights with louvered covers to mark the handsome maple treads. Downlighting focuses attention on the ebony display shelf, while providing ambient light and marking the change of direction of the stairs.
ARCHITECT: MARC RANDALL ROBINSON
DESIGN: EPIFANIO JUAREZ (JUAREZ DESIGN) AND SCOTT DESIGN—INTERIOR ARCHITECTURE & DESIGN

BEDROOMS

Once the province of glare-producing ceiling globes and fixed bedside lamps, the bedroom has since seen major improvements in lighting design. Bedroom lighting possibilities range from subtle effects to bright overall illumination. Multiple, dimmable light sources add flexibility, especially welcome in today's open, master-suite schemes.

On the subtle end of the lighting scale, soft levels create a quiet aura. Recessed downlights or tracks for reading while reclining in bed should be carefully positioned and fitted with tight trim covers and baffles or louvers to keep glare from being a problem. Decorative sconces, torcheres, or built-in cove lights can help create soft, glare-free fill light.

Bright, directional lights on either side of a double, queen-, or king-size bed allow one person to sleep while the other reads into the wee hours. Both lights should be easily adjustable and well shielded. A switch by the bed to turn off the main room light is another handy idea.

Fixtures in front of the bureau and inside closets aid in clothes selection. In walk-in dressing areas, consider the light's color temperature *(page 7)*—generally, halogen sources, with their good color rendering properties, offer the best light by which to judge clothing. Good lighting is also welcome in front of full-length mirrors, but aim the light to shine on the person, not the mirror.

This next section offers a look at the many different ways to use light in the bedroom. As you will see, many effects can be achieved, satisfying a variety of budgets and tastes.

Dramatic indirect lighting creates a relaxing atmosphere in this bedroom (near right). A strip of low-voltage mini-lights tracked underneath the bedframe help to outline it and send a glow of light onto the hardwood floor. The rice paper screen diffuses soft blue light from a spotlight with a blue filter. Another uplight glows behind the pillar, while the shimmer of the globe light at the window is gently reflected onto the warm-toned wooden chest.
**LIGHTING DESIGN:
RANDALL WHITEHEAD**

Recessed downlights and architectural cove lights provide ambient lighting in this delicately decorated bedroom (above) when daylight is kept out by wood-shuttered sliding doors. Low floor lamps on each side of the bed provide a well-directed pool of light for reading.
INTERIOR AND LIGHTING DESIGN: KENTON KNAPP, ASID, CID

ROOM-BY-ROOM LIGHTING OPTIONS   **59**

Custom European-style cabinetry frames a well-lighted headboard and alcove (right). Eyeball downlights with incandescent bulbs provide most of the light; they're controlled by dimmers built into the headboard. The brass reading lamps have dimmable switches, too, for custom light levels.
DESIGN: RUTH SOFORENKO ASSOCIATES

Translucent revolving panels define this open-plan bedroom (left) while diffusing the ambient light from a long, flush-mounted incandescent fixture behind, so that someone lying in the bed could look up without being bothered by harsh glare. An adjustable floor lamp craning over the bedside provides higher intensity light for reading.
LIGHTING DESIGN: MELINDA MORRISON LIGHTING DESIGN
ARCHITECTS: BYRON KUTH, LIZ RANIERI, AND DOUG THORNLEY (KUTH/RANIERI)

Windows on two walls provide daytime light in the warmly decorated child's bedroom above. But when the draperies are drawn or daylight falls, two brass swing-arm lamps take over to provide plenty of light for reading or playing.

In a cozy and elegant retreat, bedside lamps give off a pleasant glow reflected by gilded mirrors and the silver-painted lamp base. General room light is supplied by versatile, utlitarian tracks.
INTERIOR DESIGNER: CHER STONE BEALL (CASHMERE & COMPANY)

Lighting the way to easy clothing selection is a small track mounted high above the door in this orderly closet (left). Fitted with small fluorescent fixtures that burn cool and don't use much energy, the light is controlled by a switch on the outside of the closet.
ARCHITECT: DAVID JEREMIAH HURLEY

Recessed downlights provide ambient lighting in this elegant bedroom (below). Adjustable eyeball downlights light the display on the mantle and provide light for clothing selection in the cupboard near the door. Task light is supplied by the table lamp next to the bed, while the fireplace and candles provide warm mood lighting.
DESIGN: NICOLE PATTON INTERIORS

BATHROOMS

The number one trick to lighting bathrooms is to provide task light that's gently flattering and yet strong enough for grooming. Powder rooms offer more dramatic potential. In either case, be careful of glare around the bathtub and bouncing off mirrors. On these and the following pages are some examples of how light enhances a bathroom's decor.

Lights around a mirror used to help in shaving or applying makeup should spread light over a person's face rather than onto the mirror surface. To avoid heavy shadows, place lights at the sides, rather than only at the top of the bathroom mirror. Popular solutions include theater makeup bars and vertically mounted tubes. Some mirror units include integral tubes, inset light diffusers, or swing-out makeup mirrors with their own light source.

Fluorescent sources can make good general bathroom lighting, and are required in some energy-conscious areas. Indirect sources work well: consider cove lighting, soffit lighting, translucent diffusers, and other bounce sources that spread a soft, discreet light. Be sure to choose warm fluorescent tubes or bulbs with good color rendering properties for accurate makeup light and good skin tones.

Multiple sources and multiple controls allow you to alternate between morning efficiency and nighttime repose. Consider dimmers here, too. Also plan for low-energy night lighting for safety and convenience.

Bath and shower lights must be sealed and approved for wet locations. Any light fixture within reach of water should be protected by a ground fault circuit interrupter, or GFCI *(page 108)* installed between the service panel and bathroom.

Lighting in this master bath (left) maximizes both task and decorative opportunities. At mirrorside, a diffused inset fixture provides makeup light just where it's needed. The storage niche to the right of the mirror glows with fluorescent light passing through a diffusing panel separating open and closed storage areas.
LIGHTING DESIGN: MELINDA MORRISON LIGHTING DESIGN
ARCHITECTS: BYRON KUTH, LIZ RANIERI, AND DOUG THORNLEY (KUTH/RANIERI)

The long master bath shown above features an open fir vanity with a hand-tooled marble top. The corresponding mirror cabinet is broken by flush-mounted, vertical incandescent tubes for even makeup lighting, and the backsplash and counter areas are washed by additional light from the cabinet's bottom edge. Sunshine further brightens the room.
ARCHITECTS: BACKEN, ARRAGONI & ROSS

The bathroom at right benefits from vertical rows of incandescent bulbs flanking the vanity, as well as a curved wall of glass blocks. Clear globe fixtures (visible in the mirror) help light the shower area.
ARCHITECT: WILLIAM B. REMICK

Recessed downlights provide task lighting in front of the mirror and accent lighting in the recessed display area near the tub (below). A light strip below the glass counter adds a warm glow.
ARCHITECT: JAMES GILLAM ARCHITECTS
DESIGN: JANE NISSEN LAIDLEY

A scalloped, over-mirror soffit not only provides a unique design statement (opposite), but sheds a warm, flattering light through its diffusing glass. For fill, fiber-optic tubes run down both sides of the maple mirror cabinet; a tiny downlight highlights a nearby display niche. Additional fiber optics below the twin glass sinks and below the floor accents provide decorative touches and double as independent emergency lighting at night.
INTERIOR DESIGN: OSBURN DESIGN

A powder room offers opportunities for dramatic designs that may not be suitable for everyday use. This room (left) is awash with mirrors, glass, slate, and granite, crisply illuminated by three MR-16 downlights above the sink and another row just inside the door. The light-colored granite counter provides ample bounce light for even illumination at the sink mirror.
ARCHITECTS: BUFF, SMITH & HENSMAN
DESIGN: BOB MOORE

The graceful curve of this bathtub (right) is accentuated by the linear tile design on the side, and further underscored by the discreet lighting below the tub. The secret lies in a string of low-voltage mini-lights tucked up behind the overhang of the tub.
DESIGN: DAGMAR THIEL (KITCHEN AND BATH DESIGN)

OUTDOOR AREAS

Safety and security are important for outdoor lighting schemes, but good designs fold these into subtler, decorative landscaping plans. Beware of glare and harsh sources—it's best if light sources are indirect or hidden. If the fixtures are visible, you can control glare by placing them out of sight lines, aiming them carefully, and using shields or baffles to avoid bright spots of light. The rule of "a little light goes a long way" is especially true at night—when possible, choose multiple lower-wattage sources over a single stronger source.

The front door, areas near front walks and steps, and driveway, decks, and other outdoor spaces all have their own specific lighting requirements *(page 22)*. For example, recessed downlights or an indirect wash from accent lights works well at the front door. If the entry is well-lit, you may not need to light the front walk, but you may want to light steps, changes in direction, and any dark corners or dense shrubbery.

At night, the view from inside ends where the light ends outside. Balance light levels on both sides of a window to reduce unwanted reflections. The brightest outdoor light should be placed immediately outside the window as a transition from higher interior levels. Light levels in the middle ground should be lower, moving to soft light in the background.

Dimmers on multiple circuits help you paint a landscape to match your mood. All switches should be centrally located indoors. Timers, remote controls, and daylight-sensitive photocells are all helpful devices.

This section shows you some decorative outdoor lighting schemes that you can use as inspiration in illuminating your own outdoor areas.

These homeowners stretched indoor living space by fashioning an outdoor living room, complete with couches, spa, and a lighting scheme that's also an echo of indoor lighting. Plantings are accented with buried halogen uplights and each colorful tile cube is backlit by its own built-in light. Fluorescent wall sconces provide ambient light, two submersible pool lights highlight both the spa and the waterfall, and safety lights mark stair risers.
ARCHITECT: STEVEN ERLICH ARCHITECTS

Lights set into stair risers guide the way at night, ensuring safe footing from one level of the deck to the other. A shield over each fixture eliminates glare and directs the light down onto the treads.
ARCHITECT: KEN TATE

At night, the lights of this pool give dramatic emphasis to the bridge that links the house with the rear pool deck. Fixtures carefully tucked among plants allow light without glare.

A wooden entry deck bridges a front yard koi pond (below), glowing with submersible 120-volt lights. Striking hanging pendants with copper shields lead the way, their 150-watt reflector bulbs marking the path. Aimable uplights highlight handsome plantings; spotlights and track fixtures are tucked into eaves, downlighting foliage and filling in dark corners.
LANDSCAPE ARCHITECT: ROBERT W. CHITTOCK

The light produced by nearby entry spotlights and step lights is "recycled" through architectural panels that do triple duty as privacy screens, wind breaks, and glowing light sources along the adjacent patio. Not only do diffuse sources provide a novel decorative effect at night, but they can go a long way toward eliminating glare.
LIGHTING DESIGN: BECCA FOSTER
OWNER: DAVID HILL ASIAN ART

This handsome stone terrace can be enjoyed even after sunset, thanks to a trio of carriage lanterns spaced along the rear wall of the house. Their ornamental style nicely complements the craftsman detail of this bungalow.
ARCHITECT: RICK ARCHER (OVERLAND PARTNERS)

These elegant lanterns were designed for candlepower (right); with the addition of custom-fitted lenses and electrical wiring, they've found new life in the garden. Uplighting, provided by hidden low-voltage well-lights, seems to emanate from the lanterns as well.
DESIGN: ROSS DE ALESSI (LUMINAE, INC.)

ROOM-BY-ROOM LIGHTING OPTIONS   73

ELEMENTARY ELECTRICITY

Once you've analyzed your lighting needs and learned about the various bulbs, tubes, fixtures, and controls available (as discussed on pages 4 to 25), you're ready for the next step: improving lighting in your home. To do so, you must understand a bit about electrical circuits and wiring. Working with electricity can be relatively easy—even for the inexperienced do-it-yourselfer—provided you take the time to learn a few things about safety, codes, and electricity beforehand.

Whether you plan to simply replace a standard light switch with a dimmer, or to enhance a room with new fixtures, many of the basics are the same. These include the tools to use, circuit types, and how currents work.

In this chapter, we'll show you how electricity works, including a look at circuits *(opposite)*. Safety is discussed beginning on page 78, with information on fuses *(page 80)* and grounding *(page 81)*. Finally, starting on page 83, we'll have a look at mapping out an electrical circuit. If ever you are unsure about a procedure, or need more help, call a licensed electrician.

Properly grounding a light fixture (right) can help you avoid shock and serious injury should things go awry. For more on keeping your home's electrical system safe, see page 78.

HOW YOUR HOME IS WIRED

Utility companies distribute power to individual households through overhead wires or underground cables. Today, most homes have three-wire service. That is, the utility company connects three lines to the service entrance equipment. With this arrangement, there are two "hot" conductors (wires), each supplying electricity at 120 volts, and one "neutral" conductor. During ideal operation, this neutral wire is maintained at zero volts, or what is referred to as ground potential.

Three-wire service provides both 120-volt and 240-volt capabilities. One hot conductor and the neutral wire combine to provide for 120-volt needs, such as light fixtures or wall receptacles (outlets). Both hot conductors combine with the neutral wire to provide 120/240 volts for large appliances, such as a range or clothes dryer.

Many older homes have a limited two-wire service. These homes have only one hot conductor at 120 volts and a neutral conductor. As a result, the electrical system may not be able to handle the higher voltage requirements of an electric range or dryer.

An explanation is in order about the designation of the voltage supplied by the utility company. As mentioned on page 76, voltage is electrical pressure. Furthermore, this pressure can fluctuate from roughly 115 volts to 125 volts, even within the same day. That is why you may see references elsewhere to household voltages other than 120. This book uses 120 as the voltage between a hot line and the neutral line.

HOW DO THREE WIRES ENERGIZE YOUR HOME?

As shown below, electricity passes through a meter before it enters the service panel. Owned, installed, and serviced by the utility company, the meter is the final step in the installation of a complete wiring system. Once in place, the meter measures the electrical energy consumed in kilowatt-hours. ("Kilowatt-hours" refers to the rate of energy consumption in kilowatts

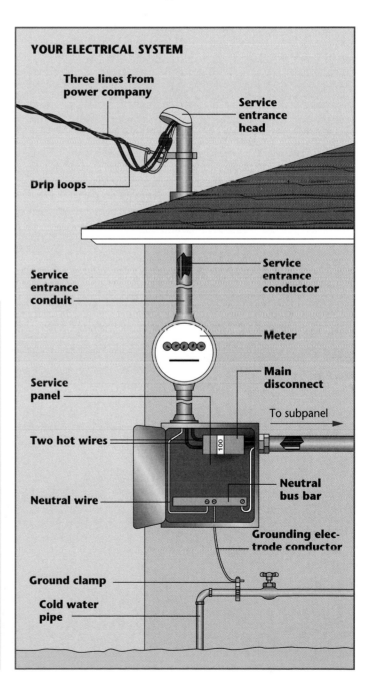

YOUR ELECTRICAL SYSTEM

- Three lines from power company
- Service entrance head
- Drip loops
- Service entrance conduit
- Service entrance conductor
- Meter
- Service panel
- Main disconnect
- To subpanel
- Two hot wires
- Neutral wire
- Neutral bus bar
- Grounding electrode conductor
- Ground clamp
- Cold water pipe

THE SERVICE PANEL

- Wires from power company
- Hot wires
- 120/240-volt circuit
- Neutral wire
- 120-volt circuits
- Hot bus bars
- Fuses or circuit breakers
- Neutral bus bar
- 120-volt circuits
- Grounding wire
- Cold-water pipe

multiplied by the time of usage in hours.) See the illustration at left on page 75 for a closer look at three-wire service.

The control center for an electrical system is the service panel, sometimes referred to as the fusebox, or panel box. This panel—a cabinet or box—usually houses the main disconnect (the main fuses or main circuit breaker), which shuts off power to the entire electrical system, and the fuses or circuit breakers that protect the individual circuits in the home.

Electricity runs from the utility company lines, through the meter, and into the service panel. Once inside the service panel it is divided into branch circuits that transmit power to the different parts of the house. Typically, each cable contains three conductors. Two hot conductors (identified by red, black, or any other color except white, gray, or green insulation) go to the main disconnect. The neutral conductor (colored white or gray) goes directly to a device called the neutral bus bar located in the service panel.

There is one other important wire associated with your service panel—the grounding electrode conductor. This conductor connects the neutral bus bar to the main water pipe in your home or to a metal ground rod driven into the ground. This safety feature provides excess current with an uninterrupted metal pathway to the ground.

SAFETY FIRST

The most important rule for do-it-yourselfers is to never work on any electrically "live" circuit, fixture, receptacle, or switch. Your life may depend on it. As well, find out about local codes—ask the electrical inspector at your building department.

Before starting work, disconnect the circuit you'll be working on at its source—in the service entrance panel, or in a separate subpanel—or by removing the protecting fuses. Switch off circuit breakers. If you've disconnected the right circuit, lights elsewhere along the circuit should not be able to be switched on.

Sometimes doing your own electrical work may not be the best idea. Check with your local building department for rules and restrictions in your area before you decide to do your own electrical work.

CURRENTS AND CIRCUITS

Electricity is a current of very tiny particles called electrons which flow on the surface of a wire. Some basic circuits are shown opposite. Some wiring terms it will help to be familiar with are defined below.

Watts: The energy consumed by the load (used by a light bulb, for instance) is expressed in watts.

Volts: The potential difference, or pressure, causing the current to flow is measured in volts.

Amperes: The intensity of current that flows through the wire or device is measured in amperes (amps). For the purposes of this book, the relationship among these units is represented in this formula: watts ÷ volts = amperes.

Path of least resistance: Another important characteristic of electric current is that it is choosy about the materials it flows through. It is partial to flowing in the path offering the least resistance. Resistance, a property of a circuit, is measured in ohms.

Conductor: The general term "conductor" applies to anything that permits, or conducts, the flow of electricity rather than resisting it. Certain materials make better conductors than others. Copper, for example, is a good conductor; most electrical wires are made of copper, although aluminum wiring is permitted in certain limited circumstances. Wires come in different gauges, or sizes; the more current, or amperes, the larger the wire required. Rubber, on the other hand, is a very poor conductor, offering so much resistance that it's often used as an insulator to prevent any flow of electricity between conductors.

THE CIRCUIT LOOP

In order to flow, electric current must have a continuous path from start to finish—like a circle. The word "circuit" refers to the entire course an electric current travels, from the source of power (like the service entrance panel or a subpanel wired to it) through some device that uses electricity (such as a toaster) and back to its starting point, the source. Each circuit forms a continuous closed path that can be traced from its source in the service panel or subpanel through

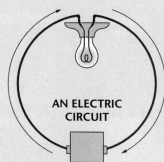

AN ELECTRIC CIRCUIT

various receptacles or appliances and back to the source.

Cables deliver electricity from the service panel to the devices on the circuit. The black wire in each cable brings electrical current to the devices, and the white wire returns the current to the service panel. Cables also contain a bare copper wire. This wire protects the entire circuit by providing a back-up pathway for electricity to return to the service panel.

Understanding Basic Circuits

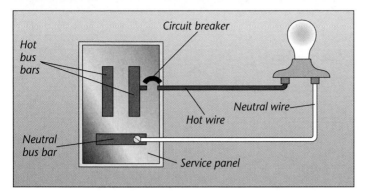

Simple circuit

A circuit is a continuous closed path in which electricity flows from the source of voltage through a device, and back to the source. In the stylized example at left, the hot wire brings electricity to a light fixture and the neutral wire returns electricity to the service panel. The white wire is connected directly to the neutral bus bar in the service panel.

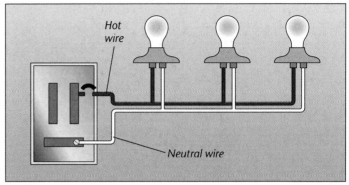

Parallel wiring

In most homes, several light fixtures operate on the same circuit using parallel wiring. In this case *(right)*, the hot and neutral wires run continuously from one fixture box to another. Wires to the individual lights branch off from these hot and neutral wires.

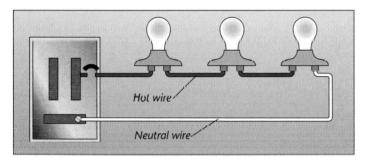

Series wiring

Often contrasted to parallel wiring is series wiring. When light fixtures are wired in series, the hot wire passes through all of the lamps before joining the neutral wire that returns to the source. Series wiring is rarely used for home light circuits because when one light bulb in the circuit fails, the rest of the lights go out. A string of old-style Christmas tree lights is an example of series wiring.

CODES AND PERMITS

The *National Electrical Code®* (referred to as "the *NEC®*" or simply "the Code") is a set of rules spelling out wiring methods and materials to be used in electrical work. With safety as its purpose, the *NEC* forms the basis for all regulations and standards applied to electrical installations. Some cities, counties, and states amend the *NEC*; check with your local building department beginning any electrical work. This book gives you the practical information you need to work within the *NEC*. In Canada, requirements may be different; consult local authorities for further information and any necessary permits.

Local utility company: Your wiring plans may involve a change in electrical service. If so, contact your local utility company to obtain the additional service. You should also contact your utility company whenever your building or remodeling plans call for changing the location of your meter and service panel, or when your project will increase your electrical load. Avoid trouble later by making sure that your utility company cables are heavy enough for your new load.

Amateur vs. professional electrician: Doing your own electrical work may not always be the best idea. A check with the building department may reveal that your jurisdiction has restrictions on how much and what kinds of electrical wiring a homeowner may do. For instance, you may be able to do all wiring up to the point at which the circuits are connected to the service panel, but the final hookup may have to be done by a licensed electrician.

If things crop up that you don't understand, or if there's some doubt remaining in your mind about your electrical system or any repairs you have done, it's best to call on a professional electrician.

National Electrical Code® and NEC® are registered trademarks of the National Fire Protection Association, Inc. Quincy, MA 02269

ELECTRICAL SAFETY

Electricity is something we all use easily with just a flick of a switch. It is also something to be treated with caution and respect. While these two statements seem to express conflicting viewpoints, together they give a good foundation for working safely with electricity. Once you understand and respect the potential hazards, electrical wiring is quite safe to do.

You can protect yourself from the risk of electrical shock by following some basic safety instructions. Before beginning to work on your wiring, always unscrew the fuse or trip the circuit breaker to the circuit involved *(page 81)*; if in doubt about which circuit to turn off, shut off the main power supply. Usually, the main disconnect is located at the service entrance panel.

WORKING SAFELY WITH ELECTRICITY

You've probably heard stories of fires or injuries from causes related to electricity. Barns burn to the ground because of electrical storms, homes are destroyed because of faulty wiring, people get electric shocks—or are killed—in household electrical accidents. You have no control over electrical storms, but you can and must be careful with electricity in your home.

Faulty wiring can cause fires. For example, the restriction of current flow through a wire or cord that is poorly connected to its plug can lead to overheating and eventually to a fire. Replace any cord or plug that shows signs of wear and tear.

Teach children not to play with cords and plugs, or to stick any object into the slots of receptacles; cap unused receptacles with safety covers that children cannot remove. See below for more on child safety.

Another fire hazard frequently found in homes is the "extension cord octopus," where too many appliances are plugged into an extension cord that isn't hefty enough to carry the electricity these appliances demand. Excessive heat builds up in the cord as it tries to carry the load for all the appliances; the cord's insulation becomes brittle or melts from the heat; the wires are exposed as the insulation deteriorates; and eventu-

---

KEEPING KIDS SAFE

Electrical outlets and cords which may pose a safety hazard to kids are commonplace in every house. Parents can't supervise a child's every move, and even children who have been warned of the dangers of electricity may be careless or take risks, so it's best to take precautions.

Electrical safety devices, such as simple outlet plugs, permanent covers, and electrical cord spools, go a long way toward assuring that kids' play is safe. These items are especially handy in homes with very young children who do not understand the potential for danger.

Permanent outlet cover

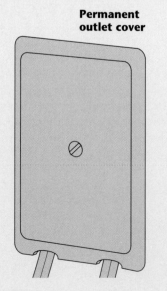

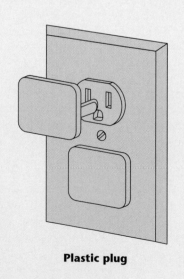

Plastic plug

Electrical cord spool

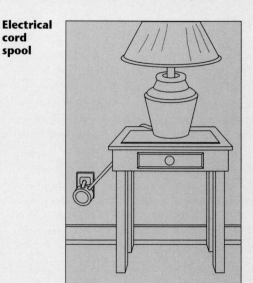

ally a short circuit develops, sending sparks flying when the bare wires touch each other.

If you notice a need for more receptacles in your home, the easiest option is to extend an existing circuit (page 92). Choose one that's not already overloaded or dedicated to a major appliance, such as a clothes dryer. Another possibility is to add a new circuit, but for this task, it's best to call an electrician.

THE CAUSE OF SHOCKS

The discussion of circuits on page 77 describes how current flows in a continuous, closed path from the source, through a device that uses power—such as a light bulb or tube—and then back to the source. If you accidentally become a link in an electrically live circuit by touching a live wire or device while simultaneously touching a grounding object or another live wire, you'll get an electrical shock.

It is important to realize that electricity doesn't have to flow in wires to make the return trip to the source. It can return to the source through any conducting body, including a person, that contacts the ground directly or touches a conductor that in turn enters the ground.

This may sound like a rather unlikely situation, but becoming the dangerous link in an electrical chain is altogether too easy. Consider that when you're partially immersed in water (such as when you're standing in a small puddle near the bathtub), touching a metal plumbing fixture, or standing on the ground on a damp concrete basement, garage, or patio floor, you're in contact with a grounded object. In other words, the first requirement of getting a shock—providing the grounding for an electrically live circuit—has been fulfilled. If you then come into contact with a live wire, the other necessary condition will be met and you will be shocked.

The only way to prevent a shock is to always ensure that the circuit you are working on is dead. As well, any circuit in use should be well grounded. See page 81 for more on grounding the system, and shutting off the power when you plan to work on the electrical system. As well, see below for more tips on electrical safety.

MORE SAFETY PRECAUTIONS

With the electricity turned off, electrical work can be performed safely. Still, it's a good idea to keep a few additional precautions in mind.

• Remember that water and electricity don't mix. Never work on wiring, fixtures, switches, or appliances in damp or wet conditions. Be especially prudent when working in basements, where the level of moisture and dampness tends to be higher than other areas of the home. Lay down dry boards to stand on if the floor or ground is wet, and wear rubber boots *(right)*.

• Leave a note on the service panel to alert others that you are working on circuit wiring. Better still—lock it.

• Study how your particular home is wired before you modify or work on the electrical system. The procedures described in this book are based on the assumption that the existing wiring was done correctly.

• Circuits are dead only past the points where they have been opened or disconnected. The lines from the utility company in the service panel are still hot, even after the fuses are removed or the circuit breakers are turned off.

• Make sure any circuit you intend to work on is dead; test to confirm the power is off before making any repairs or wire connections.

• Finally, if electrical problems crop up that you don't understand—or if there's any doubt in your mind about how to proceed with a home lighting project—it's best to call on a professional.

BUILT-IN SAFEGUARDS

Fuses and circuit breakers, collectively referred to as "overcurrent protection devices," guard electrical systems from damage by too much current.

Whenever wiring is forced to carry more current than it can safely handle—whether because of a sudden surge from the utility company, too many lights on one circuit, or a problem within the system—fuses will blow or circuit breakers will trip. These actions open the circuits, disconnecting the supply of electricity.

A circuit breaker or fuse is inserted into each circuit at the service entrance panel (or in some cases at a subpanel). For adequate protection, the amperage rating of a breaker or fuse must be the same as that of the circuit conductor it protects. For example, a circuit using #12 copper conductor has an ampacity of 20 amperes; the fuse or circuit breaker, therefore, must also be rated for 20 amperes. Never replace any fuse or circuit breaker with one of higher amperage.

A fuse contains a short strip of an alloy with a low melting point. When installed in a socket or fuseholder, the metal strip becomes a link in the circuit. If the amperage flowing in the circuit becomes greater than the rating of the fuse, the strip will melt, opening the circuit; the fuse is blown *(below)* and must be replaced.

Edison base fuses: Equipped with screw-in bases like those of ordinary light bulbs, Edison base fuses come in ratings up to 30 amps. According to the *National Electrical Code*, Edison base fuses are permitted only as replacements in 120-volt circuits. (This code restriction is meant to encourage the use of the safer Type "S" fuse.) Always match fuse size to circuit rating. For instance, if the circuit is rated for 15 amps, use a 15-amp fuse, not a 20-amp one.

Type "S" fuses: You must install the adapter with the correct rating in the fuse socket before using a Type "S" fuse. Each adapter is constructed so that it is impossible to install a fuse with a higher rating. Fuses can be replaced as needed, but once an adapter is installed, it can't be removed. Type "S" fuses are required in all new installations that use fuses to protect 120-volt circuits.

Cartridge fuses: There are two basic styles of cartridge fuses: ferrule and knife-blade. Ferrule type fuses, with ratings of 10 to 60 amps, are usually used to protect the circuit of an individual 120/240-volt appliance, such as a range. Available in ratings of 70 amps or more and suitable for 240 volts, knife-blade fuses are generally used as the main overcurrent protection in fused service entrance panels. A fuse puller *(page 87)* is best for removing cartridge fuses from their fuseholders.

Circuit breakers: Resembling a light switch, a circuit breaker serves both as a switch and a fuse. As a switch, it lets you open a circuit (by turning the switch to OFF) to work on the wiring. As a fuse, it provides automatic overcurrent protection.

When a breaker is installed in a circuit breaker panel, a bimetallic strip becomes a link in the circuit. Heat from excessive current will bend the metal strip, causing a release to trip and break the circuit. (The toggle goes to OFF or to an intermediate position when this happens.)

Unlike fuses which self-destruct, circuit breakers can be reset once they've tripped. Breakers are rated for a specific amperage. As with fuses, a breaker's amp rating must match the ampacity of the circuit it protects.

The service panel: Though the ultimate capabilities are usually the same, the exact location and type of service equipment vary from home to home. The service panel is usually on an inside wall, often directly behind the meter, but it might be on the outside of your home, below the meter *(page 75)*. It might have only one main disconnect, or as many as six switches controlling disconnection. Also, the service entrance panel may or may not contain branch circuit overcurrent protection devices. Some systems have subpanels after the main service entrance panel; these contain the overcurrent protection devices for the branch circuits. Variations also occur in the type of overcurrent protection device. Some systems use circuit breakers; others use fuses. However, the principles of safety and protection are the same regardless of the location and type of service equipment.

A GALLERY OF FUSES AND CIRCUIT BREAKERS

Edison base fuse

(Top view)

Good fuse

Blown fuse

Type "S" fuse

Cartridge fuses

Ferrule type

Knife-blade type

Single-pole circuit breaker

GROUNDING THE SYSTEM

As a preventive measure, electrical codes require that every 120-volt circuit has a grounding system. This assures that all metal parts of a circuit which a person might accidentally touch are maintained at zero voltage, because they are connected directly to the ground.

In a typical house circuit, the wiring method dictates how grounding is done. When a home is wired with armored cable, or metal conduit, the conductive metal enclosures can themselves form the grounding system.

When metal enclosures are not used, a separate grounding wire must be run with the circuit wires. Running a separate grounding wire isn't as complicated as it may sound because nonmetallic sheathed cable (called NM cable) contains a bare grounding wire *(page 88)*.

During normal operation, the grounding system does nothing. However, in the event of a malfunction, the grounding is there for your protection. See the following page for more on safeguarding against shock.

SHUTTING OFF POWER

Most service panels have a switch or switches that can disconnect the entire electrical supply instantly. This shut-off mechanism, also called the "main disconnect," is a vital safety feature whenever you work on existing wiring or make major repairs, or in case of an emergency, such as a fire.

When shutting off power to a circuit at the service panel, spend another moment to prevent a possible disaster. As a safety measure, tape a note on the panel explaining what you're doing so no one will come along and replace the fuse or reset the circuit breaker while you're working on the wiring. Then either carry the fuse in your pocket, tape the circuit breaker in the OFF position, or lock the service panel.

One final step is to check that the circuit is actually dead—a neon tester plugged into a receptacle on the circuit shouldn't glow, and a lamp shouldn't work.

The illustrations below show some typical main disconnects, usually identified as "Main" on the service panel. Killing power to a circuit is similarly discussed.

Lever disconnect
An external handle controls contact with two main fuses in the cabinet. When you pull the handle to the OFF position, the main power supply is shut off.

To remove a plug fuse in the service panel to work on one circuit, find the fuse controlling the appropriate circuit. Grasp the fuse by its insulated rim and unscrew it. Check that electrical devices on the circuit are dead. If not, you have removed the wrong fuse.

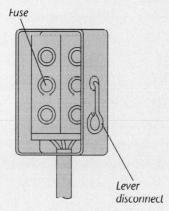

Fuse

Lever disconnect

Single main circuit breaker
Switching the main breaker to the OFF position shuts off all power.

To shut off an individual circuit, locate the breaker protecting the circuit to be shut off, then push the toggle to the OFF position. To reset a tripped breaker, flip the toggle to ON. Many modern breakers go to an intermediate position when tripped. To reset, switch the toggle first to OFF, then ON.

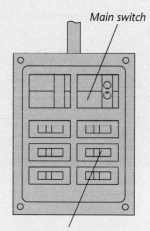

Main switch

Circuit breaker

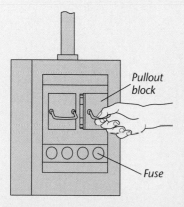

Pullout block

Fuse

Pullout block
The main cartridge fuses are mounted on one or two nonmetallic pullout blocks. By pulling firmly on the handgrips, you can remove the blocks from the cabinet and disconnect all power.

Removing a cartridge fuse is similar: First locate the fuse block—which resembles a pullout block—protecting the circuit you wish to shut off. Pull out the block, grasping the handle firmly. Use a fuse puller or your hand to release the cartridge fuse from the spring clips.

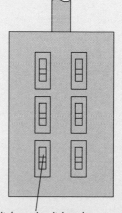

Switch or circuit breaker

Multiple main circuit breakers
Some older homes do not have a single main disconnect. One half of the panel (usually the top) contains a number of breakers that constitute the main. All must be must be switched to OFF to disconnect all power. Single-pole switches are sometimes installed in the main (top) section, even though this is not legal. It is potentially dangerous, since these circuits remain live even if all main circuit breakers are switched to OFF. Contact an electrician to rectify the situation.

Grounding to Avoid Shock

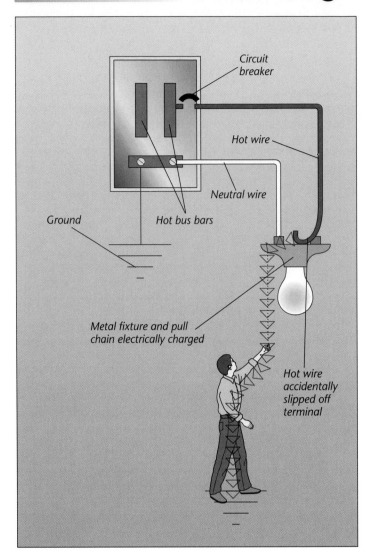

Circuit breaker

Hot wire

Neutral wire

Ground

Hot bus bars

Metal fixture and pull chain electrically charged

Hot wire accidentally slipped off terminal

Creating a short circuit

If, for instance, a hot wire accidentally became dislodged from a fixture terminal and came into contact with the metal canopy of the light fixture, the fixture and pull chain would become electrically charged, or "hot." If you were to touch the chain or fixture under these conditions, a short circuit could occur in which you would provide the path to ground for the electric current. In other words, you would get a shock *(left)*. (See page 79 for more on the cause of electrical shocks.)

A short circuit could occur in any number of places where electricity and conductive materials are together—in power tools and appliances with metal housings; in metal switch, junction, and outlet boxes; and in metal faceplates.

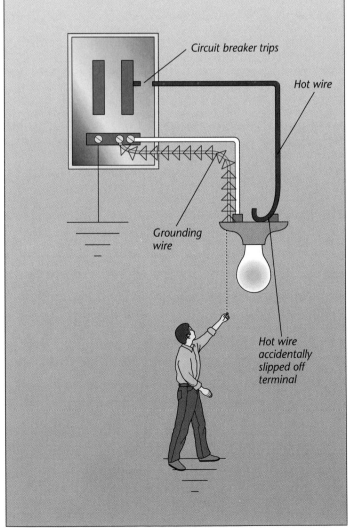

Circuit breaker trips

Hot wire

Grounding wire

Hot wire accidentally slipped off terminal

Preventing electrical shocks

The shock in the example shown above could have been prevented if the circuit had had a grounding system as shown at right. A grounding wire connecting the neutral bus bar to the metal housing of the light fixture would provide an auxiliary electrical path to ground in the event of a short circuit. This grounding wire would carry the fault current back to the distribution center and assure that the fuse or circuit breaker protecting the circuit would trip, or open, shutting off all current flow. See page 81 for more on grounding the electrical system.

CIRCUIT MAPPING

What do I have to work with? This is the first question you should ask yourself when you consider any repairs, alterations, or additions to your present electrical system. Mapping out your electrical circuit, and knowing how to determine the electrical load that lighting fixtures and other appliances place on your system are equally important.

The first step in evaluating your electrical system is to determine what type of service you have. Looking through the glass window of your electricity meter, you'll probably see several numbers printed on the faceplate (if not, call your utility company for this information). The designation "120V" indicates two-wire service; "240V" indicates three-wire service with both 120-volt and 240-volt capabilities.

INDIVIDUAL CIRCUITS
Once you've established your service rating, you should make a list of all light fixtures, switches, and appliances on each circuit. The illustration on the following page shows how to map your home's wiring. If the circuits are not identified on the service panel or if you suspect that the labeling may be incorrect or out of date, take the time to enter the correct information so you'll be able to kill power to the right circuit when you need to.

SERVICE RATINGS
Any electrical system is rated for the maximum amount of current (measured in amperes) it can carry. This rating, determined by the size of the service entrance equipment, is called the "service rating." Keeping you within the bounds of your service rating is the job of the main fuses or circuit breaker.

Service ratings have increased through the years to accommodate greater electrical demands and higher safety standards. Today, the average service rating

of most new homes is 200 amps. Depending to a large extent on the age of your home, your service rating could be as low as 30 amps or as high as 400 amps. In between the two extremes are the following common service ratings: 60, 100, 125, 150, and 200 amps.

The best way to find out your service rating is to look at the main disconnect, if you have one. Whether it is a breaker or fuses, the service rating will usually be stamped in clear view.

If your system doesn't have a main disconnect, or if you are unsure, call the utility company or your local building inspection department rather than trying to figure out the service rating yourself. Someone from either of those two offices will be able to help.

RATINGS OF LESS THAN 100-AMP SERVICE
If your service rating is less than 100 amps, you can't use the formula given in the table on page 85 to calculate your load. You can, however, use a different formula that incorporates the same *NEC* values for typical usage. Therefore, the general purpose circuits, small appliance circuits, and laundry circuits are computed exactly as they are in the first three entries of the table.

Once you have figured out the general purpose circuit load (3 watts x number of square feet of living area), add 1,500 watts for each 20-amp small appliance circuit and laundry circuit. Using this total, take the first 3,000 watts at 100 percent and the balance over 3,000 watts at 35 percent: [3,000 + 0.35 (total - 3,000)].

Add to this value the nameplate rating of all major appliances (space heater, garbage disposal, dishwasher, etc.). This gives your estimated load in watts. Sample wattages are provided on page 85. Find the current by dividing the total wattage by your voltage—120 volts for two-wire service or 240 volts for three-wire service.

POINTS TO REMEMBER WHEN TESTING CIRCUITS

- Make sure the lamp or fixture that you use for testing works and is turned on.
- Make sure to test both ends of a duplex receptacle.
- Don't forget to test the switches on any garbage disposal units or dishwashers.
- Once the 120-volt circuits are charted, go on to the 240-volt circuits. These circuits, identified in your service

panel by a double circuit breaker or a pull-out fuse block with cartridge fuses, go to individual high-wattage appliances such as an electric range, clothes dryer, water heater, heating system, or central air conditioner. Trace the 240-volt circuits by disengaging one overcurrent protection device at a time and finding out which appliance doesn't work.

Using numbers and electrical symbols, you can make up a good working drawing of your electrical system. Such a drawing or map can save you much time, whether you plan to alter existing wiring, troubleshoot a problem or even wire a new home. The following is a circuit map of a typical two-bedroom house. Note that the dashed lines indicate which switch controls which fixture; they do not show wire routes.

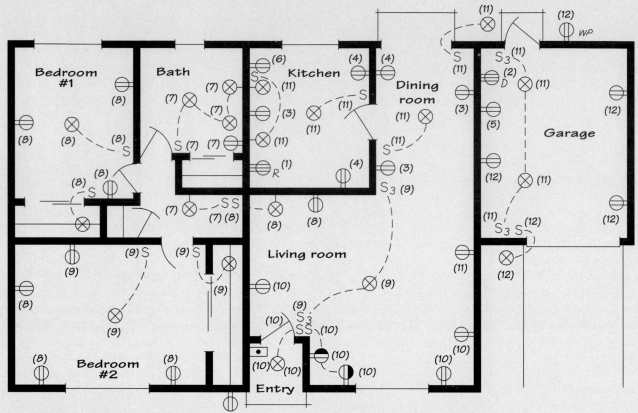

1. Range (240-volt circuit)
2. Dryer (240-volt circuit)
3. Kitchen and dining room
   20 amp
4. Kitchen and dining room
   20 amp
5. Washer
   20 amp
6. Dishwasher
   20 amp
7. Bath and hall
   15 amp
8. Bedroom #1
   15 amp
9. Bedroom #2
   15 amp
10. Living room
    15 amp
11. Living room
    15 amp
12. Garage
    20 amp

ELECTRICAL SYMBOLS

⊗   Light fixture

⊖   Duplex receptacle

⊖   Duplex receptacle, half controlled by switch

S   Single-pole switch

S_3 Three-way switch

⊖R   Range outlet

⊖D   Dryer outlet

▲   Special outlet

▣   Doorbell

⊖WP   Weatherproof receptacle

——   Switch wiring

After mapping out the wiring, the next step is to determine your present usage, or electrical load. The *National Electrical Code* has established certain values that represent typical electrical usage.

Some wattage requirements of common household items are shown below. As well, a formula for calculating electrical load is provided—allowing for a nominal value of 1,500 watts for each 20-amp small appliance circuit. Use three watts per square foot of living space for general purpose circuits (general lighting and receptacles).

Air conditioner, central	5,000
Air conditioner, room	800-1,600
Blender	350-1,000
Can opener	100-216
Coffee grinder	85-132
Coffee maker	850-1,625
Computer	125-200
Computer printer	125-200
Dishwasher	1,080-1,800
Drill, portable	360
Dryer, clothes	5,600-9,000
Fan, ceiling	150
Fan, exhaust (for range)	176
Fax machine	125-200
Food processor	200
Freezer, standard	720
Furnace, fuel-fired	800
Garbage disposal	300-900
Hair dryer, hand-held	260-1,500
Heater, built-in (baseboard)	1,600
Lamps, fluorescent (per bulb)	5-110
Lamps, halogen (per bulb)	20-500
Lamps, incandescent (per bulb)	25-250
Microwave oven	975-1,575
Mixer, portable	150
Radio	100
Range, oven	4,000-8,000
Refrigerator, frostless	960-1,200
Sander, portable	540
Saw, circular	1,200
Steam iron	1,100
Stereo, compact disc player	12-15
receiver	420
Telephone answering machine	10-12
Television, color	300
Toaster	800-1,600
Trash compactor	1,250
Vacuum cleaner	250-800
VCR	17-23
Washer, clothes	840
Water heater	4,000-6,000

Applying these values to your own home, and using the nameplate values of appliances, you can use one of several formulas to calculate your electrical load. One such formula—for homes with 120/240 volt service of 100 amps or more—is presented as a worksheet below.

Compare the calculated load with your present service rating *(page 83)*. The rating should be higher than the value calculated. If the two values are close, your present service cannot accommodate the addition of new loads; extend your circuit *(page 92)* or have a new one added.

How to estimate your electrical load (for 120/240-volt service of 100 amps or more):

_____ sq. ft. of living area (outside dimensions)
× 3 watts per sq. ft. =   _____ watts

_____ 20-amp small appliance circuits
× 1,500 watts =   _____ watts

Example: Laundry circuit (1,500 watts)_____ watts

Appliance nameplate values (if values are given in amps, multiply by volts to get watts)

water heater	_____ watts
dryer	_____ watts
dishwasher	_____ watts
garbage disposal	_____ watts
range	_____ watts
trash compactor	_____ watts
other	_____ watts
Add all entries. Total =	_____ watts

Take 40% of the amount over 10,000 watts:
Subtract 10,000 watts.   −10,000 watts
difference =   _____ watts
0.40 × difference =   _____ watts

Find subtotal by adding 10,000 to
amount computed above.   +10,000 watts
subtotal =   _____ watts

Air conditioner or heater(s) (whichever has the largest value)   _____ watts

Add the last two lines.
YOUR ESTIMATED LOAD =   _____ watts

Convert load to current by dividing by 240 volts.
estimated load in
watts ÷ 240 volts =   _____ amps

WIRING IT ALL TOGETHER

Now that you are familiar with lighting products and basic wiring concepts, you'll want to know the specifics of adding lighting to your home. Obviously, wiring is an essential part of this process.

With only a few tools and materials, and the proper know-how, you can modify or add lighting to any area of your property—both indoors and out. Most of these processes are fairly simple, but don't hesitate to contact an electrician if you have any doubts about your abilities.

The chapter begins with a look at the tools required for the job *(opposite)*. On page 88, we'll introduce some materials common in home lighting procedures. Working with wire—including splicing—begins on page 89. If you need to extend a circuit, turn to page 92 for help. For information on using surface-mounted fixtures, downlights, and track systems, turn to pages 96, 97, and 99, respectively. Page 100 begins with a look at working with receptacles, and page 102 opens the discussion of switches. Finally, to find out how to light up the outdoors, turn to page 106.

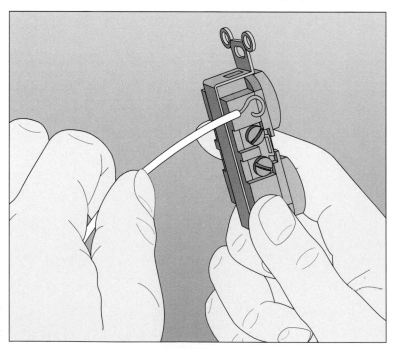

Whether you're installing a receptacle or a switch, you'll need to attach wire to screw terminals (above). For details, turn to page 91.

SOME USEFUL TOOLS

You can handle most wiring for lighting and other electrical repairs in the home with the specialized tools shown below. Many of these tools, such as diagonal-cutting pliers, lineman's pliers, and wire strippers, make it easier and safer to prepare wire ends, and to make sound wire connections at lamp sockets, switches, receptacles, and other electrical devices. The versa-

tile multipurpose tool strips insulation from wires, and its blades slice through wire. It also can be used to attach crimp connectors to wire ends. A fish tape is indispensable if you are planning to route wire behind existing walls, ceilings, or flooring. Always use a neon tester to confirm that power to the circuit is off before beginning any electrical work *(page 89)*.

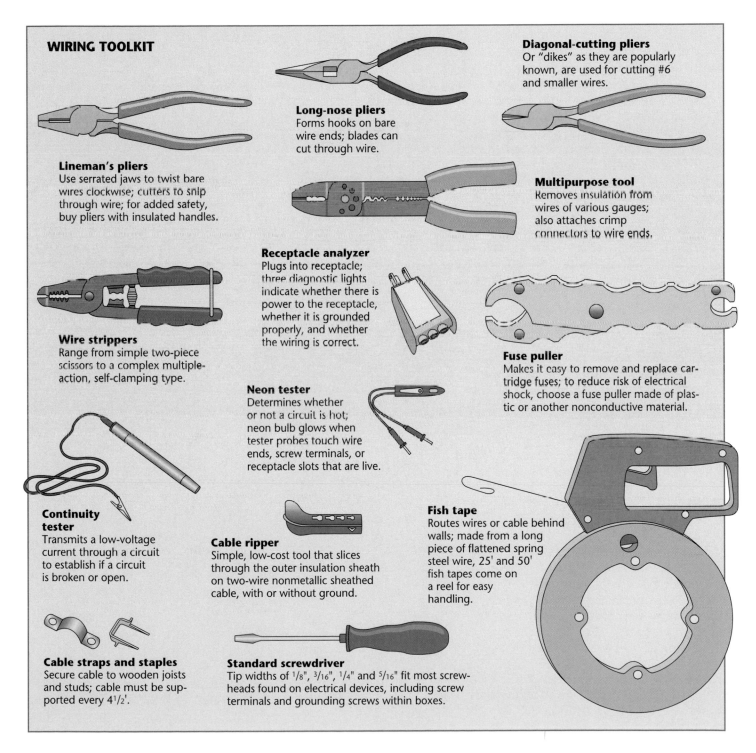

WIRING TOOLKIT

Lineman's pliers
Use serrated jaws to twist bare wires clockwise; cutters to snip through wire; for added safety, buy pliers with insulated handles.

Long-nose pliers
Forms hooks on bare wire ends; blades can cut through wire.

Diagonal-cutting pliers
Or "dikes" as they are popularly known, are used for cutting #6 and smaller wires.

Multipurpose tool
Removes insulation from wires of various gauges; also attaches crimp connectors to wire ends.

Wire strippers
Range from simple two-piece scissors to a complex multiple-action, self-clamping type.

Receptacle analyzer
Plugs into receptacle; three diagnostic lights indicate whether there is power to the receptacle, whether it is grounded properly, and whether the wiring is correct.

Fuse puller
Makes it easy to remove and replace cartridge fuses; to reduce risk of electrical shock, choose a fuse puller made of plastic or another nonconductive material.

Neon tester
Determines whether or not a circuit is hot; neon bulb glows when tester probes touch wire ends, screw terminals, or receptacle slots that are live.

Continuity tester
Transmits a low-voltage current through a circuit to establish if a circuit is broken or open.

Cable ripper
Simple, low-cost tool that slices through the outer insulation sheath on two-wire nonmetallic sheathed cable, with or without ground.

Fish tape
Routes wires or cable behind walls; made from a long piece of flattened spring steel wire, 25' and 50' fish tapes come on a reel for easy handling.

Cable straps and staples
Secure cable to wooden joists and studs; cable must be supported every 4$\frac{1}{2}$'.

Standard screwdriver
Tip widths of $\frac{1}{8}$", $\frac{3}{16}$", $\frac{1}{4}$" and $\frac{5}{16}$" fit most screwheads found on electrical devices, including screw terminals and grounding screws within boxes.

BASIC WIRING MATERIALS

There are standard components in any home's electrical setup. A few of the essentials are discussed below and illustrated at right.

CABLES, WIRES, AND CONDUCTORS

Cable consists of two or more wires contained in the same protective outer sheathing. A single conductor is a wire, usually insulated. A grounding wire may be bare, particularly when contained within a cable.

American Wire Gauge (AWG) numbers indicate the diameter of the wire—not including the insulation—and appear on the sheathing and on individual wires.

Cable is identified by the size and number of conductors it contains. A cable with two #14 wires and a grounding wire is called a "14-2 with ground"(right). Nonmetallic sheathed cable—which includes NM cable (right) and UF cable for outdoor circuits (page 106)—is used in most residential wiring. Type AC, metal-clad cable, and flexible conduit can also be used for indoor projects, but should be installed by a professional.

Single conductors (individual wires) are shielded by color-coded, nonconducting thermoplastic. Neutral wires are white or gray, grounding wires are green, and hot wires are all other colors (red, black, etc.).

To ensure the best connection, use only cable containing all-copper wire, not aluminum or copper-clad aluminum wire. If you must attach copper wire to existing aluminum wire, contact your local building official for advice on how to safely do so.

CONNECTORS AND HOUSING BOXES

Wire nuts join and protect the stripped ends of spliced wires within housing boxes (right). They are sized to accommodate various wire combinations. Some jurisdictions require compression sleeves for grounding wires because they provide a more permanent bond than wire nuts. If in doubt, contact your local building department.

Housing boxes provide connection points inside walls or ceilings—either for splicing wires or for mounting fixtures, switches, or receptacles. Metal boxes are stronger than plastic, but require grounding.

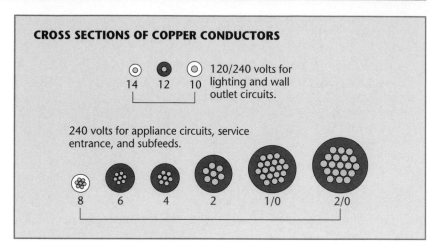

CROSS SECTIONS OF COPPER CONDUCTORS

14 12 10 120/240 volts for lighting and wall outlet circuits.

240 volts for appliance circuits, service entrance, and subfeeds.

8 6 4 2 1/0 2/0

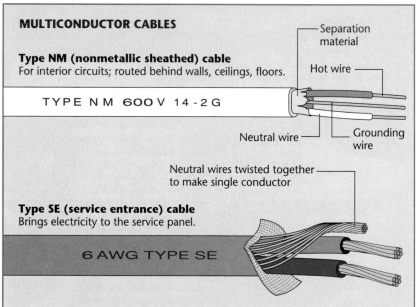

MULTICONDUCTOR CABLES

Type NM (nonmetallic sheathed) cable
For interior circuits; routed behind walls, ceilings, floors.

TYPE NM 600V 14-2G

Separation material

Hot wire

Neutral wire

Grounding wire

Neutral wires twisted together to make single conductor

Type SE (service entrance) cable
Brings electricity to the service panel.

6 AWG TYPE SE

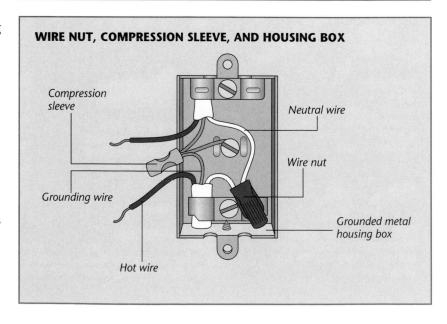

WIRE NUT, COMPRESSION SLEEVE, AND HOUSING BOX

Compression sleeve

Neutral wire

Wire nut

Grounding wire

Grounded metal housing box

Hot wire

WORKING WITH WIRE

To properly wire lighting circuits—including stripping, securing, and splicing wire—you must first learn some basic techniques. These are described in an easy-to-follow manner over the next pages.

Before connecting a cable to a device or joining it to another cable, cut open and remove the outer sheath, cut away all separation materials, and strip the insulation from the ends of the individual conductors.

To lay open a cable *(page 90)*, such as two-wire NM cable, use a cable ripper or knife. With round, three-wire cable—such as for three-way switches—a pocket, linoleum, or utility knife is best so you can follow the rotation of the wires without cutting into their insulation. Always rest cable on a flat board or wall surface, and cut in the direction away from your body.

Use a wire stripper or the graduated wire stripper jaws on a multipurpose tool to peel off a wire's outer insulation *(page 90)*. Use a pocket knife for larger wires (#8 to #4/0). Strip a length of wire a bit longer than needed in case you nick the wire. If this happens, snip off the nicked end, otherwise it could break off—especially since the nick is usually where the wire is bent to form a loop for a connection to a screw terminal *(page 91)*.

Wires are joined together (spliced) with solderless, mechanical connectors *(page 91)*. These are of two basic types: wire nuts and compression sleeves. However, if you must splice aluminum wire to copper wire, use a special two-compartment connector.

First test that the circuit you'll be working on is dead, as described below.

TESTING

Two basic diagnostic tools are available to help in electrical work. They are the neon tester, shown here, and the continuity tester, illustrated on page 87.

Neon tester: Use this to confirm that the circuit is dead before you touch bare wire ends. Be careful: you may be near live wires. Always hold the probes by their insulation. A carelessly placed probe can cause a short circuit if it accidentally touches both a hot and a grounded object at the same time.

To confirm that a circuit is dead using a neon tester, grasp the leads by their insulated handles, then touch one probe to a hot wire or terminal and the other to a neutral wire or terminal, to the equipment grounding conductor, or to the grounded metal box. The tester will light if the circuit is hot.

To find the hot wire of a two-wire circuit with ground *(right)*, touch one probe to the grounding wire or metal box and touch the other probe to the other wires, one at a time. The tester lights when the second probe touches the hot wire.

When a lamp or appliance doesn't work, the neon tester can determine whether it's because the appliance is faulty or the circuit is dead. Insert the probes into the slots of a receptacle; if the tester lights up, the circuit is fine.

Continuity tester: There are several different kinds—one includes a battery and light, another uses a battery and a buzzer

or bell—but all are battery-powered. These devices send a low-voltage current through a circuit to determine if there is damage to an electrical path, such as when the path is broken, or when a short circuit exists.

Make sure the power is off before using a continuity tester. At the service panel, either turn off the breaker or pull the fuse *(page 81)*.

A continuity tester can be used to check electrical devices such as a cartridge fuse, switch, socket, or wire. If the tester lights or buzzes, the device is sound. To test a cartridge fuse, first remove the fuse from the fuse block *(page 81)*. Touch the tester probes to each end of the fuse. If the fuse is good—current flows properly—the tester will light or buzz.

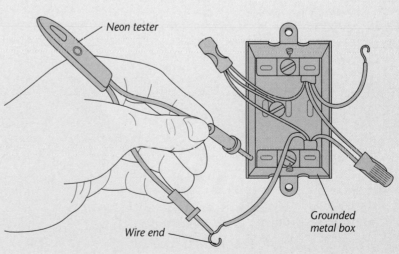

Neon tester

Wire end

Grounded metal box

Stripping Cable and Wire

Cable consists of insulated and bare wires bundled together and wrapped in an outer sheath of insulation. Stripping cables and individual wires is a simple process, as shown below.

In the course of home lighting maintenance and repair, you may occasionally need to make connections with stranded wire from lamp and other lighting fixture cords. See below and opposite for more.

Special tools, such as a wire stripper, a multipurpose tool, or a cable ripper, are used to strip a wire's insulation or a cable's protective thermoplastic coating. For cable, once you've cut off the outer sheath and any separation materials, strip the insulation off wire ends. With lamp cords, the strands which make up each wire are delicate—always use wire strippers to remove the insulation.

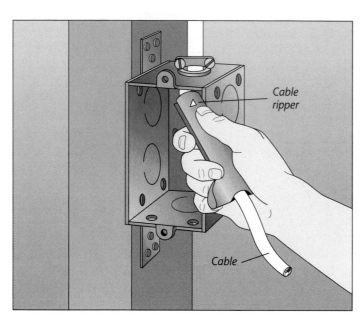

Cable ripper

Cable

Stripping cable
To remove the outer insulation from a cable, slide a cable ripper up the cable to the top of the box *(left)*. Press the handles of the cable ripper together and pull toward the end of the cable. This will score the outer sheath. Bend the cable back to crack the score and then peel open the outer sheath of insulation.

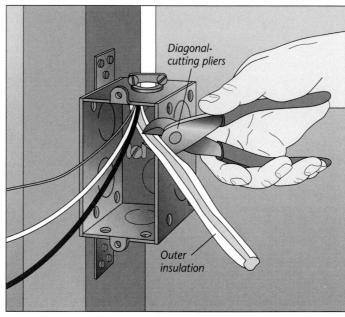

Diagonal-cutting pliers

Outer insulation

Cutting off cable insulation
Separate the wires from the insulation *(right)*. Using a pair of diagonal-cutting pliers, cut off the opened outer sheath of insulation and all separation materials.

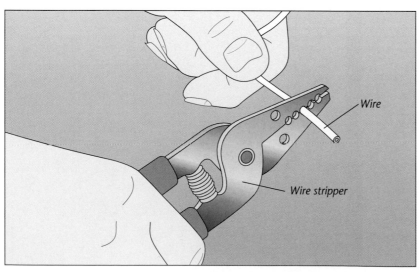

Wire

Wire stripper

Stripping wire
Using a wire stripper, insert the wire into the matching slot *(left)*, or set the adjustment screw for the gauge of wire. Holding the wire firmly in your hand with your thumb extended toward the end of the wire, position the stripper on the wire at an angle and press the handles together. Rock the stripper back and forth until the insulation is severed and can be pulled off the wire. For joining individual wires, about 1" of insulation must be stripped off the ends. To make wire-to-screw-terminal connections, strip about 1/2" to 3/4" of insulation off the wire end. When working with stranded wire—commonly found in lamp cords—strip about 3/4" of insulation from the wire end using wire strippers.

Securing and Splicing

Preparing wire ends and securing a terminal connection

Using long-nose pliers, form a two-third to three-quarter loop in the bare wire. Starting near the insulation, bend the wire at a right angle and make progressive bends, moving the pliers toward the wire end until a loop is formed. Hook the wire clockwise around the screw terminal *(right)*. As you tighten the screw, the loop on the wire will close. If you hook the wire backward (counterclockwise), tightening the screw will tend to open the loop.

When working with stranded wire from a cord—usually there are two or more wires together in a cord—twist the exposed strands in each wire together tightly in a clockwise direction. To attach the wire to a screw terminal, shape the twisted strands into a loop and hook it around a screw terminal in a clockwise direction. Tighten the screw, making sure that no stray wire ends are exposed.

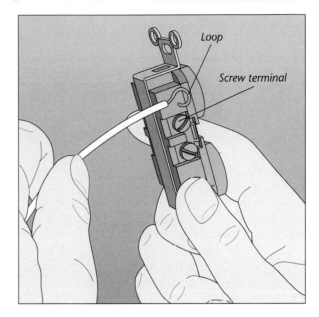

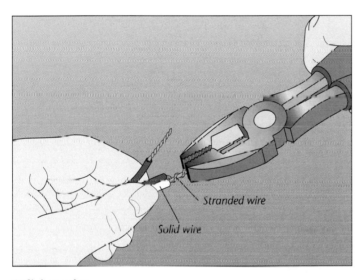

Splicing wire

To attach stranded cord wire to a solid wire, first strip insulation from both stranded wire ends, as described opposite, then twisting them each tightly in a clockwise direction. Position the two wire ends so that they are parallel to each other and wrap the stranded wire around the solid wire in a spiral fashion *(above)*. To secure the splice, fold the exposed wire ends using lineman's pliers and screw on a wire nut.

For joining individual wires, the action of screwing on the wire nut twists the wires together. Holding the wires parallel, screw a wire nut on clockwise until it is tight and no bare wire is exposed.

If you are securing spliced wires with a compression sleeve, twist the wire ends clockwise at least one and one-half turns. Snip 3/8" to 1/2" off the twisted ends so that they are even. Slip a compression sleeve onto the wire ends, and crimp the sleeve using a multipurpose tool. Put on an insulating cap. When used to connect grounding wires, a compression sleeve need not be covered with an insulating cap.

MAKING A PIGTAIL SPLICE

This arrangement is nothing more than three or more wires spliced together. One of the wires (the pigtail) connects to a terminal on an electrical device such as a switch or receptacle. The pigtail wire, usually 6 inches long, must match the gauge of the other wires in the splice. A wire nut or a compression sleeve is used to secure the splice. Electrician's tape should never be used in place of a wire nut. Tape is useful for emergency insulation repairs, but it's not a substitute for a good mechanical splice.

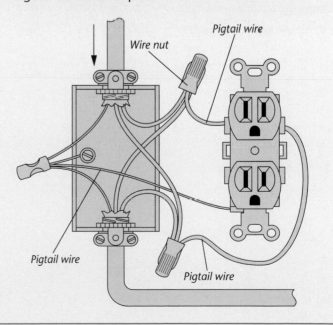

EXTENDING A CIRCUIT

Your lighting project may call for adding a new fixture, switch, or receptacle to an already-existing electrical circuit. On the pages that follow, we present techniques for extending a circuit using nonmetallic sheathed cable, type NM *(page 88)*.

Once you've decided which circuit you will tap into, you will need to choose a housing box. The information below and on the facing page will help you make your choice. When you're ready to connect the new lighting devices, turn to page 96.

SELECTING A POWER SOURCE

A circuit can be tapped wherever there's an accessible outlet, switch, fixture, or junction box. The only exceptions are when you have a switch box without a neutral wire or when there's a switch-controlled fixture at the end of a circuit.

Because of code restrictions, you must tap the correct type of circuit. You should also ensure that the intended circuit doesn't already carry the maximum electrical load allowed. See page 83 for more information.

Before deciding where to tap the circuit, consider how you'll route wire to the new fixture, switch, or

receptacle. Examine your home's construction, looking for the easiest paths behind walls, above ceilings, and under floors.

The box tapped must be large enough to accommodate the new wires and must have a knockout hole through which you can thread the new cable. If the source is accessible but the box isn't right, replace it with one of the many types on the market *(opposite)*.

CAUTION: Before working on any existing box or device, disconnect the proper circuit by removing the fuse or switching the circuit breaker to OFF.

PREPARING FOR NEW BOXES

After selecting the proper power source, but before routing the cable, you must buy the right boxes, determine where to put them, and cut holes for them in the walls or in the ceiling.

Choosing boxes: For switches and outlets and for fixtures that weigh 24 ounces or less, consider cut-in or plain boxes, which can be secured in the spaces between studs or joists. For heavier fixtures, use boxes that can be anchored to studs or joists.

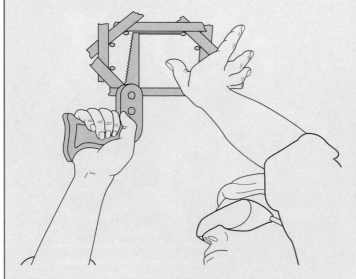

Many recessed fixtures come prewired to their own housing boxes. For more about fixtures, see page 96.

Selecting a box location: To locate a box in a wall or ceiling, you'll need to determine the positions not only of studs and joists but also of any obstructions, such as pipes or wires. CAUTION: Before you do any work, be sure to shut off power to all circuits that might be wired behind the wall or ceiling.

Drill a small test hole where you want the box. Then bend a 9" length of stiff wire to a 90° angle at the center, push one end of the wire through the hole, and turn it. If it bumps into something, move over a few inches and try again until you find an empty space.

When locating a box on a plaster-and-lath wall, chip away enough plaster around the test hole to expose a full width of lath. Plan to center the box on the lath.

Cutting the hole: Trace the box's outline on the wall or ceiling, omitting any protruding brackets from your outline. To cut the box hole, drill pilot holes in the corners of the outline then, with a keyhole saw *(left)* or saber saw, cut along the outline. If you're cutting through plaster, first apply masking tape to the outside border of your outline to prevent the plaster from cracking. Brace a plaster ceiling as you cut.

WORKING WITH NEW BOXES

Boxes are connection points, either for joining wires or for connection to devices such as receptacles, switches, and fixtures. Regardless of general trade terminology, most boxes are interchangeable in function. For example, with appropriate contents and covers, the same box could be used as an outlet box, a junction box, or a switch box.

The variety of sizes and shapes corresponds to differences in wiring methods, kinds and number of devices attached to the box, and number of wires entering it. Boxes can be either metal or nonmetallic. Metal is sturdier but must be grounded, whereas nonmetallic boxes cost less and don't require grounding. Most new plastic boxes—made of tough nylon—are fairly strong, unlike the old, breakable fiber boxes.

Electrical boxes for rewiring work come in many types. Sometimes called "old-work" or "cut-in" boxes, these mount easily where wall and ceiling coverings are already in place—unlike new-work boxes.

Before you mount a new housing box, remove a knockout for each new cable. NM cable must be secured to a metal box either with built-in cable clamps or with a separate metal cable connector. Cable need not be clamped to a single-unit nonmetallic box if the cable is stapled within 8 inches of the box; if you can't staple, use a box with built-in clamps. But cable must be clamped to ganged boxes. Let cable extend 6 to 8 inches into the box for making connections.

How you mount the new box will depend on its type. You can mount boxes either on the wall or ceiling. Several examples are shown in the illustrations at right.

For example, to secure wall cut-in boxes, tighten the screw behind the box.

For a ceiling box with flange, check the box's fit in the hole; then nail or screw the flange to the side of the joist or stud.

Adjustable hanger bars are used to secure ceiling boxes when there is access from above the ceiling, but fan rated spreader bars are used when there is no access from above. In this case, install the bar through the ceiling opening made for the box.

To mount a pancake box, simply screw this box to the bottom of a joist or hang it from a hanger bar.

WALL AND CEILING BOXES

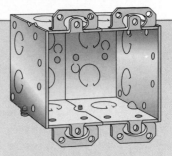

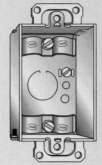

Plain box
Adjustable ears allow this wall box to be mounted in wooden and plaster-and-lath walls. When a box is screwed directly on a wooden wall, the faceplate hides the ears.

Ganged box
Removable sides allow two of these wall boxes to fit together, forming a box large enough to hold more than one device.

Junction box
When an outlet box contains only wire splices or cable connections—no devices—it's topped with a plain cover and referred to as a junction box. Mount this type (left) on the wall.

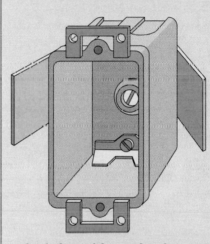

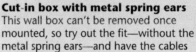

Nail-on handy box
These nonmetallic wall boxes are convenient for side-mounting.

Cut-in box with metal spring ears
This wall box can't be removed once mounted, so try out the fit—without the metal spring ears—and have the cables in place beforehand.

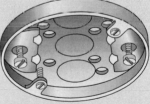

Pancake box
Flat enough to attach directly to a ceiling's hanger bar or to a joist; accommodates one two-wire cable.

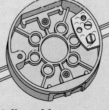

Adjustable hanger bar
Attaches to two joists, supporting ceiling fixture box; install where you have access from above ceiling.

Ceiling box with flange
Nails directly onto ceiling joist; good choice where you have access from above ceiling.

Routing Cable

Routing cable where there's access

If you have access through an unfinished attic or basement, routing cable is relatively easy. Routing cable for a new receptacle via an unfinished attic is shown at right. First, make a hole for the box in the open space between studs; then drill a $^3/_{16}$" guide hole up through the ceiling into the attic to mark the location. In the attic, locate the guide hole and drill a $^3/_4$" hole next to it down through the top plates for the cable to run through.

To make sure there's nothing blocking your path, have a helper hold a flashlight in the box hole while you look down through the hole in the top plates. If you can't see the beam from the flashlight, a fireblock or some other obstruction is in the way. You'll probably have to cut away the wall covering and notch or drill through the block.

Once the path is clear, run a fish tape through the cable hole, then feed it down the inside of the wall. Open the hooked end on another fish tape and feed it through the box hole, wiggling it around until it snags the hook on the first tape. Pull both fish tapes through the box hole, then disconnect them. The hooked end of the fish tape that descends from the attic will be sticking out of the hole.

Strip 8" of sheathing from one end of the new cable, then secure its wires to the fish tape with electrician's tape. Back in the attic, pull on the fish tape to pull the cable through the box hole and up into the attic, where you can then run it to the rest of the circuit.

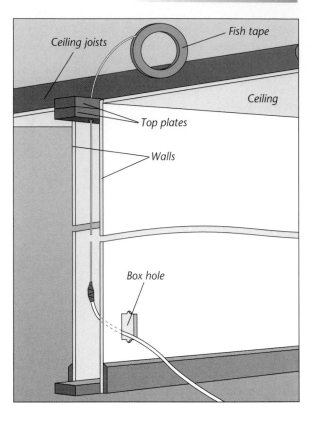

Ceiling joists — Fish tape — Ceiling — Top plates — Walls — Box hole

Routing cable where there's no access

If you don't have access via an unfinished space, you'll have to cut away wall, ceiling, or floor coverings. Some materials, such as ceramic tile or plaster walls, are more difficult to patch than gypsum wallboard and should be left alone where possible. In some cases, it's best to rely on the services of a professional.

As shown in the illustration at left, when you don't have access, you'll have to cut a number of holes through the wall or ceiling (or both, depending on exactly what you're wiring) and fish the cable from hole to hole. First cut the holes you'll need for the fixtures, switches, and receptacles. Aligning them vertically under each other makes running cable easier. Then, cut extra access holes as necessary, such as at the junction of the ceiling and the wall, and close to the floor. Running the cable close to the floor allows you to conceal the work behind the baseboards. Cut a channel in the wall to run the cable through. You'll need to secure the cable to the wall studs with metal plates since all cable installed less than $1^1/_4$" from a finished surface must be protected by a $^1/_{16}$" metal plate where it passes through or in front of supports (studs or joists).

Fish the cable from hole to hole using two fish tapes, as described above for routing cable with access. Remember to leave enough cable projecting from the various holes to make the connections required. Once you've fished cable to all new sites, finish installing the fixtures, switches, and receptacles before patching holes and reinstalling any baseboards.

Ceiling joists — Fish tape — Fixture box hole — Ceiling-wall hole — Switch box hole — Power source — Access hole — Cable — Channel

Tapping Into a Circuit

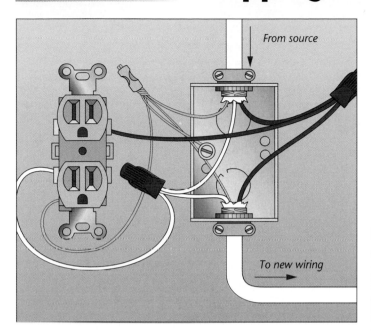

From source

To new wiring

How to wire into a receptacle

De-energize the circuit *(page 81)* and gently pull the receptacle from the box. Secure the two white (neutral) wires from the cables together with a white jumper wire attached to a silver screw terminal and screw on a wire nut, as shown at left. Repeat the procedure for the black wires, attaching the jumper to a brass screw terminal. Using a compression sleeve, secure the new grounding wire together with the other grounding wires and a jumper wire to the box.

In some areas, direct wiring to the screw terminals on the receptacles is also allowed. Check with your local building department for regulations in your area.

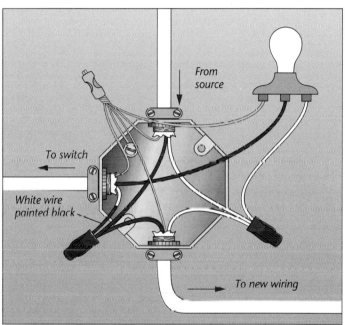

From source

To switch

White wire painted black

To new wiring

How to wire into a fixture

Pull the fixture from the box and confirm that the power is off *(page 81)*. Connect the wires of the new cable as shown above.

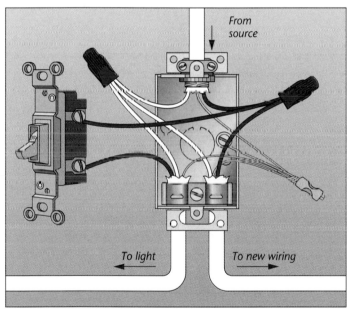

From source

To light

To new wiring

How to wire into a switch

Pull the switch from the box and use a neon tester to locate the hot black wire *(page 89)*. Turn off power to the circuit. Follow the procedure for wiring into a receptacle, taking care to secure the black wire from the new cable to the hot wire.

How to wire into a junction box

Remove the cover from the junction box and confirm that the power is off. The illustration at right shows a typical wiring extension from an existing junction box.

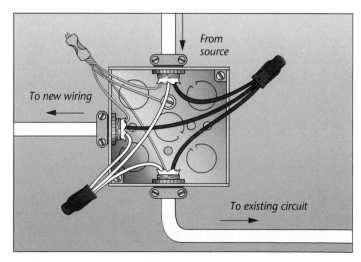

From source

To new wiring

To existing circuit

FIXTURES

Wired-in fixtures, whether surface-mounted or recessed, are all installed in basically the same way. The fixture is fastened to the housing box and the wires coming from the cable are attached to those of the fixture. Recessed fixtures are trickier to install in an existing ceiling. They're easier to install in new construction or below an unfinished attic or crawl space.

Over the next four pages, we'll discuss various types of fixtures, and provide installation instructions for downlights (*page 98*) and track systems (*page 99*).

SURFACE-MOUNTED FIXTURES

The size and weight of the fixture determine the mounting method. New fixtures usually come with their own mounting hardware, which is adaptable to any standard fixture box.

Grounding metal fixtures: The *National Electrical Code* requires that all incandescent and fluorescent fixtures with exposed metal parts be grounded. Even if the fixture box itself is grounded, the fixture attached to it won't necessarily be grounded. A suspended fixture needs a grounding wire run from the socket to the box. Most new fixtures are prewired with a grounding wire.

If the fixture box is not grounded, such as when the house wiring has no grounding wire, extend a grounding wire from the box to the nearest cold-water pipe. To do this, wrap one end of a length of #12 copper wire around the grounding screw or the screw holding the fixture to the box. Secure the other end to a grounding clamp (available in different sizes for different-sized pipes) fastened to the pipe.

Replacing a fixture: Disconnect the circuit (*page 81*), then remove the old fixture's cover, if any. Unscrew the canopy from the fixture box; detach the mounting bar if one exists. Have a helper hold the fixture to

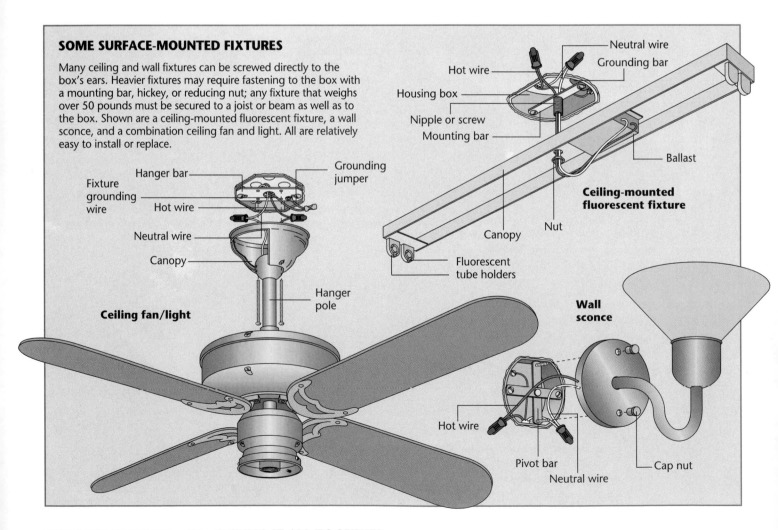

SOME SURFACE-MOUNTED FIXTURES

Many ceiling and wall fixtures can be screwed directly to the box's ears. Heavier fixtures may require fastening to the box with a mounting bar, hickey, or reducing nut; any fixture that weighs over 50 pounds must be secured to a joist or beam as well as to the box. Shown are a ceiling-mounted fluorescent fixture, a wall sconce, and a combination ceiling fan and light. All are relatively easy to install or replace.

Neutral wire
Grounding bar
Hot wire
Housing box
Nipple or screw
Mounting bar
Ballast

Ceiling-mounted fluorescent fixture

Canopy
Nut
Fluorescent tube holders

Hanger bar
Grounding jumper
Fixture grounding wire
Hot wire
Neutral wire
Canopy
Hanger pole

Ceiling fan/light

Wall sconce

Hot wire
Pivot bar
Neutral wire
Cap nut

keep it from falling, or hang the fixture with a short piece of coat hanger wire from the mounting strap to the mounting hole in the fixture.

Disconnect the wires by either unscrewing the wire nuts and untwisting the wires, or unwinding the electrical tape. Lay the old fixture aside.

Strip 1/2 inch of insulation from the new fixture's wires. Then, as your helper—or coat-hanger wire—holds up the new fixture, splice the new wires to match the arrangement of the old ones, covering the splices with wire nuts *(page 91)*. Secure the new fixture by reversing the steps you took to remove the old one, using any new hardware included.

Adding a new fixture: Route the cable from the power source *(page 94)*, and install switch and fixture boxes. Then follow the steps for replacing a fixture.

New nonmetallic cable routed to the box should include a grounding wire attached to the box's grounding screw *(below, left)*. If more than one cable enters the box (a separate cable may be connected to the switch box), attach the end of a grounding jumper (a short length of #12 wire) to the grounding screw and splice its other end to the ends of the grounding wires in the cables *(below, right)*. Cap the splice with a compression sleeve.

Nonmetallic boxes don't need grounding, but you'll have to ground the fixture. Choose a box with a metal grounding bar. For a fixture at the end of a circuit, attach the cable grounding wire to the bar. For a fixture in the middle of the circuit, join the cable grounding wire to the bar with a grounding jumper. All grounding wires on a new fixture should be properly attached to a grounding system.

To install the fixture, match the box's wires to those of the fixture—black wire to fixture hot wire, white wire to fixture neutral wire. If the fixture has a separate grounding wire, join it to the grounding wires in the box. Cap all splices with wire nuts. Mount the fixture with the hardware specified by the manufacturer.

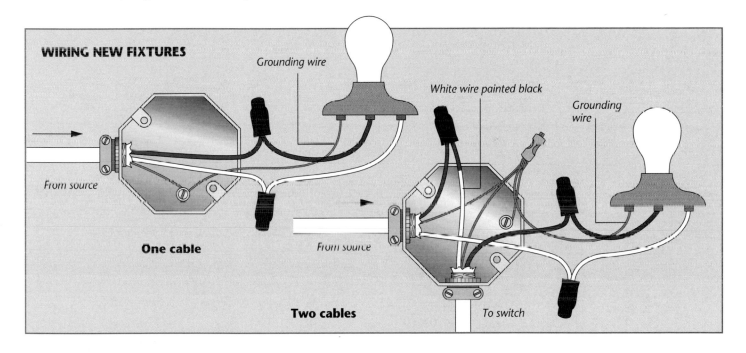

WIRING NEW FIXTURES

Grounding wire

White wire painted black

Grounding wire

From source

One cable

From source

Two cables

To switch

DOWNLIGHTS

Today, recessed downlights are usually prewired and grounded to their own housing box; older-style downlights, though, must be wired into a junction box attached to a joist.

Many downlights produce a lot of heat, so remove insulation within 3 inches of the fixture or buy an "IC" rated fixture for direct contact. Make sure that no combustible materials are within 1/2 inch, with the exception of joists or other blocking used for support. Most low-voltage downlights have an integral transformer attached to the frame. If not, mount an external transformer nearby, then route wire to the fixture.

Before installing the fixture, you'll need to cut a hole for the fixture housing in the ceiling between two joists. If there's no crawl space above the joists, locate the joists—and any obstructing wires or pipes—from below using the bent-wire method described on page 92; be sure to shut off power to any circuits that might be wired behind the ceiling before drilling exploratory holes.

Once you've located a suitable place for the housing, you'll need to trace its outline on the ceiling, then cut the hole with a keyhole saw or saber saw. See the following page for more on installing downlights.

Installing Downlights

Downlight with box

Use the diagram at right to guide you when installing a downlight with its own box. With this type, the fixture and its box are pre-mounted on a metal frame.

Downlights with adjustable hanger bars are easy to install from above—you probably won't even need a helper to do it. Simply nail the ends of the bars to joists on either side; then clip the fixture trim or baffle into place from below.

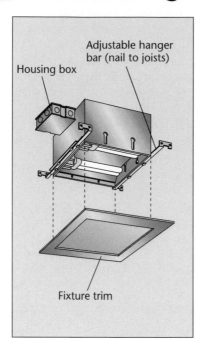

Housing box
Adjustable hanger bar (nail to joists)
Fixture trim

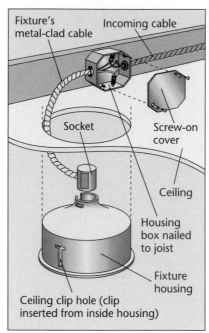

Fixture's metal-clad cable
Incoming cable
Socket
Screw-on cover
Ceiling
Housing box nailed to joist
Fixture housing
Ceiling clip hole (clip inserted from inside housing)

Downlight without box

To connect this type of fixture to incoming cable, you must select a housing box that can be nailed to a ceiling joist, as shown at left. After clamping and wiring the fixture's cable into the housing box, gently snap the fixture housing into its socket. Then push the fixture into place and secure it to the ceiling material using clips. The metal-clad cable grounds the fixture to the box.

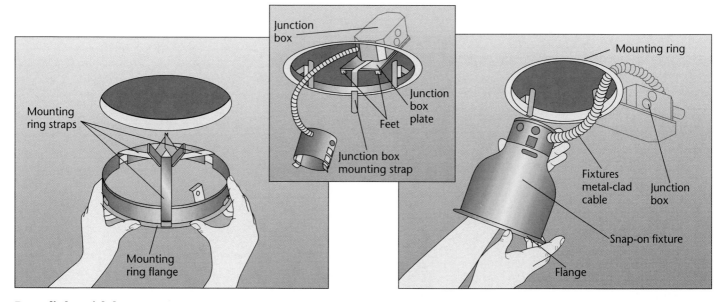

Mounting ring straps
Mounting ring flange
Junction box
Junction box plate
Feet
Junction box mounting strap
Mounting ring
Fixtures metal-clad cable
Junction box
Snap-on fixture
Flange

Downlight with box—no access

If you don't have easy access to the area where you want to install the downlight, look for a commercially available "remodeling" fixture. Installation procedures vary among manufacturers but the basics are the same. One model is shown here, but be sure to follow the instructions that come with the model you choose.

Cut a ceiling hole large enough to fit the mounting ring; slip the ring through *(above, left)* until the flange sits against the ceiling and secure it with the mounting straps. Some models will require that you wire the junction box and push it through the opening before attaching the mounting ring. Otherwise, you can temporarily hang the junction box from the mounting ring to assist with the wire in.

Open the junction box and feed the incoming NM cable into it through a knockout hole. Attach the white fixture wire to the white

(neutral) cable wire, the black fixture wire to the black (hot) cable wire, and the bare fixture wire to the cable's grounding wire, securing each connection with a wire nut or compression sleeve. Place all electrical connections in the junction box, making sure that they won't interfere with the ability of the cable clamp to provide strain relief, and close the cover. Next, insert the junction box mounting strap between the ceiling material and the mounting ring, and through the junction box slot on the mounting ring. Pull the strap down until the junction box plate sits flat on the ceiling with the feet over the edge of the ceiling thickness *(above, middle)*. Then, bend the mounting strap up to secure the box in position.

Finally, snap the fixture into position *(above, right)* and push it into the hole until its flange is flush against the ceiling.

Installing Track Systems

Track systems are mounted, either directly or with mounting clips, to the wall or ceiling. Power is provided either by a plug-in connector or by directly wiring the fixture into the system. For greatest flexibility, tracks can be wired into two (or more) circuits and controlled by different switches.

Low-voltage track fixtures with integral transformers or adapters can be plugged into a standard 120-volt track, as shown below *(top)*.

Generally, this type would be used when extensive rewiring is not desired or permitted—such as in apartments, or in certain areas where the local code prohibits it. It can also be a quick fix for a particular lighting concern, such as highlighting artwork.

An external transformer can also be used to step down power to the track itself. First mount the transformer and then route wire to the track location. An advantage of this wire-in method *(below, bottom)* is that it minimizes costs: one transformer can serve many fixtures, so each fixture is cheaper.

When you attach a track to the ceiling or wall, you'll use mounting screws or toggle bolts in predrilled holes. To determine the positions of the necessary holes, hold the track in place against the wall or ceiling and mark the positions of the knockout holes. These marks show you where to drill.

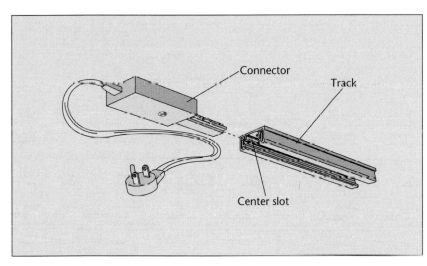

Connector

Track

Center slot

Plug-in connector and track

A plug-in connector, which includes a cord and a lamp plug, lets you place a track wherever the cord will reach an outlet. In lieu of plugging and unplugging the light, plug-ins can also be controlled using snap switches attached to the cord, like those used for some lamps. The connector is mounted flush against the wall or ceiling so that you can attach the track directly to the wall or ceiling. Hold up the first length of track (you may need a helper), join the end to the connector, and secure the track to the ceiling or wall using mounting screws or toggle bolts. Attach the remaining lengths of track in the same way. Note that plug-in connectors can be used only with single-circuit tracks.

Wire-in connector and track

A track system with a wire-in connector is hooked up directly to a housing box. Whether you use an existing box or install a new one, you'll need as many wall switches as your track has circuits. If you're simply replacing a fixture with a single-circuit track system, you can use the existing wall switch. By using a special connector called a floating canopy available with some track systems, you can bring in power along a track run rather than at the end. To install a wire-in connector, position the fixture box saddle and then splice the connector's wires to the incoming cable wires. Cap each splice with a wire nut. Some connectors attach to the fixture box saddle; others are simply held in place by the track. You may need special clips to hold the track 1/4" to 1/2" away from the mounting surface. Screw or bolt the clips to the ceiling or wall; then slip the first length of track onto the connector. Press it, and succeeding lengths, into the clips.

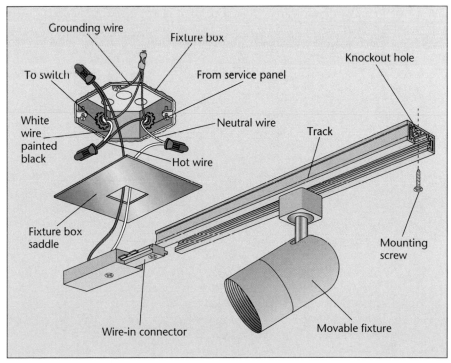

Grounding wire

Fixture box

Knockout hole

To switch

From service panel

White wire painted black

Neutral wire

Track

Hot wire

Fixture box saddle

Wire-in connector

Mounting screw

Movable fixture

RECEPTACLES

Grounded receptacles consist of an upper and lower outlet with three slots. The larger (neutral) slot accepts the wide prong of a three-prong plug; the smaller (hot) slot is for the narrow prong, and the U-shaped grounding slot is for the grounding prong. Code requires that all receptacles for 15- or 20-amp, 120-volt branch circuits (most of the circuits in your home) be of the grounding type shown below. Like switches *(page 102)*, all receptacles are rated for a specific amperage and voltage and stamped with this information. Be sure to buy what you need.

Screw terminals: Receptacles have three different colors of screw terminals. The brass-colored screws, on one side of the receptacle, are hot terminals; the white- or silver-colored screws, on the opposite side, are neutral terminals; and the green screw is the grounding terminal.

Wiring options: The *National Electrical Code* accepts various wiring connections: direct connection of hot and neutral wires to the screw terminals; use of jumper wires between the receptacle and the hot and neutral wires of the incoming and outgoing cables; and backwiring *(below)*. Not all of these possibilities are accepted in all areas. Check with your local building department before you begin.

Backwired receptacles: Some receptacles have holes on the back into which you can insert wires. Black wires go in the holes located on the same side as the brass-colored screws, and white wires in holes on the same side as the silver-colored screws. A wire gauge on the back shows how much insulation to strip off the wire ends. The grounding wire must still be attached to the green screw terminal on the receptacle.

240-volt receptacles: To eliminate the possibility of plugging a 120-volt appliance into a 240-volt receptacle, higher-voltage circuits use special receptacles and matching attachment plugs.

Wiring configurations: Receptacles can be wired in a number of ways depending on where they're located in the circuit. When replacing an existing receptacle, you can determine its location in the circuit by counting the number of cables entering the box—first remove the faceplate and pull the receptacle from the box. When two or more cables enter the box, the receptacle is in the middle of the circuit; one cable brings power to the receptacle; the other cable sends power to the next box on the circuit. When only one cable enters the box, the receptacle is at the end of the circuit. Receptacle wiring also differs if the receptacle is controlled by a switch—such as for receptacles at the end of the circuit. Use caution and be sure to double-check connections.

The diagrams on the facing page show typical wiring configurations for receptacles in the middle and at the end of the circuit, as well as a split-circuit receptacle with one half wired to a switch. Use them as a reference when you are installing a receptacle. When you are replacing a defective receptacle, take note of its wiring configuration before you detach the wires.

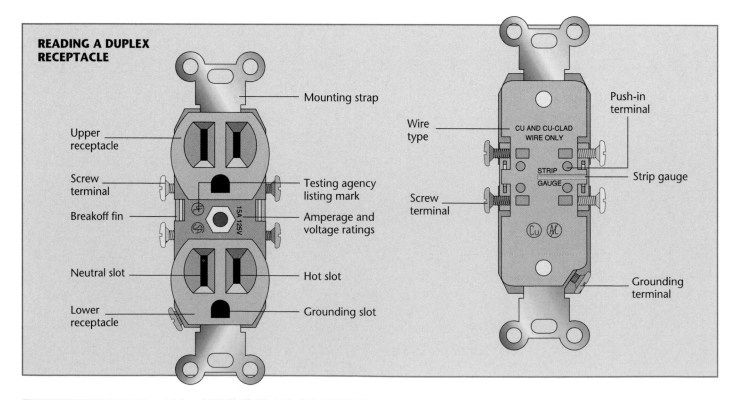

READING A DUPLEX RECEPTACLE

Mounting strap

Upper receptacle

Screw terminal

Breakoff fin

Neutral slot

Lower receptacle

Testing agency listing mark

Amperage and voltage ratings

Hot slot

Grounding slot

15A 125V

Wire type

Screw terminal

CU AND CU-CLAD WIRE ONLY

STRIP GAUGE

Cu   AL

Push-in terminal

Strip gauge

Grounding terminal

Wiring Receptacles

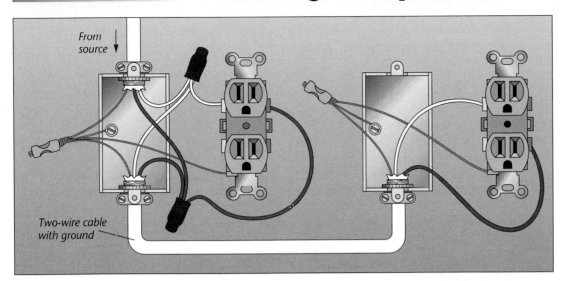

From source

Two-wire cable with ground

Receptacle at the end of the circuit
In this example *(left)*, the receptacles are wired parallel to each other in the same circuit. Both the upper and lower outlets of each receptacle are always hot.

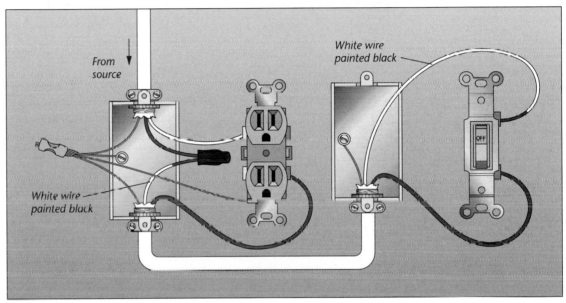

Switch-controlled receptacle
Both the upper and lower outlets of this receptacle *(right)*, located at the end of a circuit, are controlled by a single-pole switch. When the switch is in the ON position, the receptacle is hot; when the switch is turned off, the receptacle does not receive power.

From source

White wire painted black

White wire painted black

Tab removed here

From source

Split-circuit receptacle
In this example *(left)*, the metal tab connecting the upper and lower outlets has been removed, thus allowing the outlets to operate independently. One outlet of this duplex receptacle is always hot, while the other half is controlled by a switch. When the switch is in the ON position, power flows to the outlet.

SWITCHES

All switches are rated according to the specific amperage and voltage for which they are suited. Switches marked CO-ALR can be used with either copper or aluminum wire. Unmarked switches and those marked CU can be used with copper wire only. Never mix copper and aluminum wiring, unless by approved means, because the way in which the different metals conduct electricity will cause the wire connection to heat up.

Whether you are replacing an old switch or adding new ones to your home, read the information stamped on your new switch carefully. Make sure the switch you are going to install has the same amperage and voltage ratings as the one you are replacing, or that it is suitable for the circuit.

Switches are screwed to boxes by their mounting straps. Always install the switch completely vertical even if the box is crooked.

Most switches in a home are of the single-pole or three-way variety. Single-pole switches have two terminals of the same color and a definite right side up. All switches are wired into hot (black) wires only. In general, this means that the normally neutral white wire will be recoded black because it is now hot—but this is not specifically required by the Code. This will always be the case at the end of a circuit, sometimes called a "switch loop." With a single-pole switch, it makes no difference which hot wire goes to which terminal.

Three-way switches have two terminals of the same color (brass or silver colored) which are often called traveler terminals, and one of another color (usually black) which is often called the common terminal or point. There is no right side up or upside down with a three-way switch; however, it is important to know which of the three terminals is the odd-colored one.

The switches shown on these pages have no grounding terminals—the grounding wires from the cables are pigtailed to the grounding screw on a metallic box. When installing a nonmetallic switch box at the end of a circuit, secure the end of the grounding wire between the switch bracket and the mounting screw. Switches with grounding terminals may be available at greater expense, and they may be required in some regions—contact your local building department for information. For this type of switch simply attach the grounding wire to the terminal.

There are many specialty switches available—such as timers and time-delay switches—which control a fixture without you needing to be there. These can be used for home security and convenience. Shown below is a dimmer switch which conserves electricity while allowing you to control the light's brightness. Specialty switches generally have two hot wire leads instead of terminals.

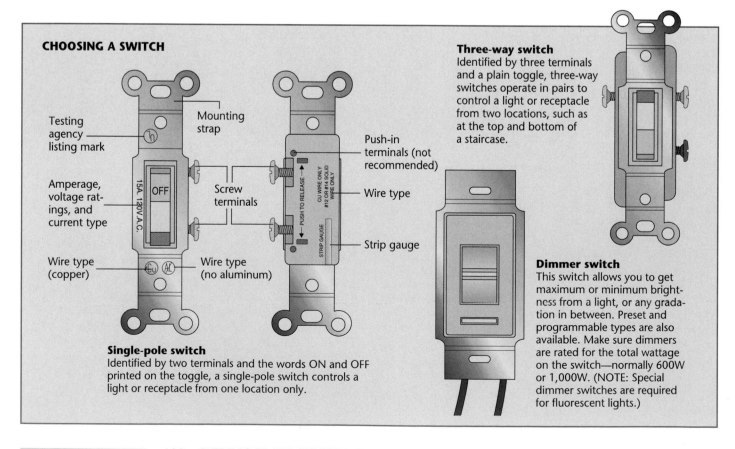

CHOOSING A SWITCH

Testing agency listing mark

Amperage, voltage ratings, and current type

15A. 120V.A.C.

OFF

Wire type (copper)

Mounting strap

Screw terminals

Wire type (no aluminum)

PUSH TO RELEASE

CU WIRE ONLY #12 OR #14 SOLID WIRE ONLY

STRIP GAUGE

Push-in terminals (not recommended)

Wire type

Strip gauge

Single-pole switch
Identified by two terminals and the words ON and OFF printed on the toggle, a single-pole switch controls a light or receptacle from one location only.

Three-way switch
Identified by three terminals and a plain toggle, three-way switches operate in pairs to control a light or receptacle from two locations, such as at the top and bottom of a staircase.

Dimmer switch
This switch allows you to get maximum or minimum brightness from a light, or any gradation in between. Preset and programmable types are also available. Make sure dimmers are rated for the total wattage on the switch—normally 600W or 1,000W. (NOTE: Special dimmer switches are required for fluorescent lights.)

Light controlled by a switch

The illustration at right shows a light fixture controlled by a single-pole switch. Notice that the black (hot) wires are attached directly to the screw terminals on the switch; the neutral wires bypass the switch and go directly to the light fixture.

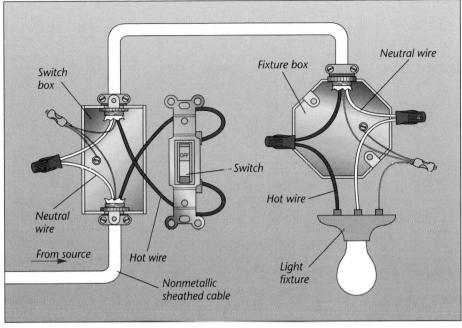

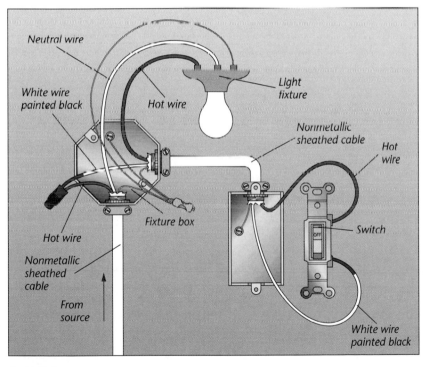

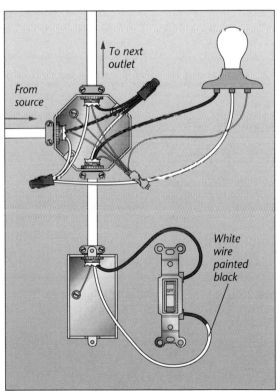

Switch loop

Because of code limitations on the number of wires that a given size box may contain, circuit wires sometimes run to the light first, with a switch loop going to the switch. This situation is illustrated above. The black (hot) wire in the cable connects to both the light and the switch. The white wire is also hot and is recoded black in this example, although this is not required by the Code—check electrical guidelines in your area.

Light in the middle of the circuit

In this example (above), the light is in the middle of a circuit (two or more cables enter the box), and the switch is wired in a switch loop. The switch controls the light in the middle of the circuit run.

Wiring Three-way Switches

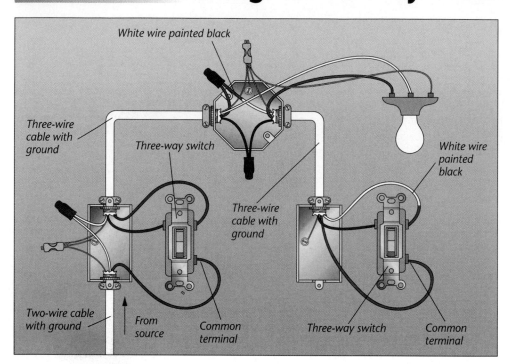

White wire painted black

Three-wire
cable with
ground

Three-way switch

Three-wire
cable with
ground

White wire
painted
black

Two-wire cable
with ground

From
source

Common
terminal

Three-way switch

Common
terminal

End of the circuit

A light is wired between a pair of three-way switches. CAUTION: Check the location of the common terminal on the switch (it will be marked); if it is different from this example (*left*), connect the black (hot) wire that runs between the switches to the common terminal on each switch. Three-wire cable has an extra hot red wire and is used between the switches.

THREE-WAY SWITCHES

If you want to be able to turn a light on and off at two locations, such as at the top and the bottom of a staircase or at either end of a hallway, consider installing a pair of three-way switches.

Though single-pole and three-way switches look somewhat alike, two features distinguish them. A single-pole switch has two terminals for wire connections and the words "ON" and "OFF" embossed on the toggle. A three-way switch, on the other hand, has three terminals; "ON" and "OFF" are not indicated on the toggle, since the on and off positions may change, depending on the position of the other switch.

In order to clarify the action of three-way switches, the illustrations at right show a pair of them in a simple light circuit. Each switch has three terminals and a movable blade. The light is off when the circuit is open, one switch is up and one down (*right, top*). Flip either switch so both are up or down (*right, bottom*), and the circuit is completed; the light is on.

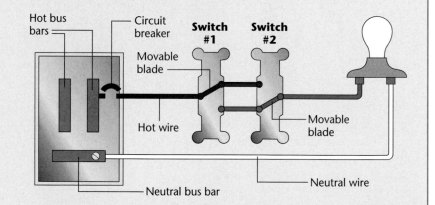

Hot bus
bars

Circuit
breaker

Switch
#1

Switch
#2

Movable
blade

Hot wire

Movable
blade

Neutral bus bar

Neutral wire

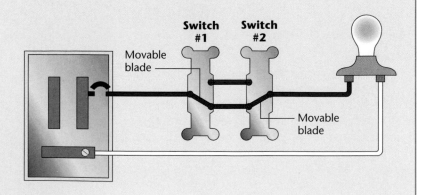

Switch
#1

Switch
#2

Movable
blade

Movable
blade

Installing Switches

Preparing the wires

Turn off power to the circuit at the service panel *(page 81)*. If you are replacing a switch, unscrew the faceplate, pull the switch out of the box, then check to confirm that the circuit is dead. Detach the wires from the old switch.

If you are installing a new switch, install the box *(page 93)*. Then, secure the cables to the box so that 6" to 8" of each cable extends from the box, past the front edge. Strip the outer sheath of insulation from the cables *(page 90)*, removing the sheath and all separation materials. Strip off ¹/₂" to ³/₄" insulation from each wire *(right)*.

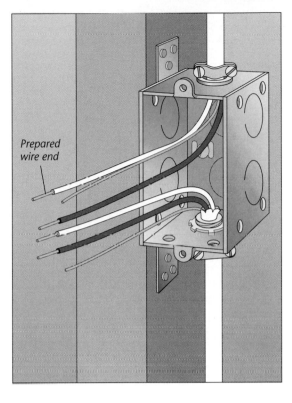

Prepared wire end

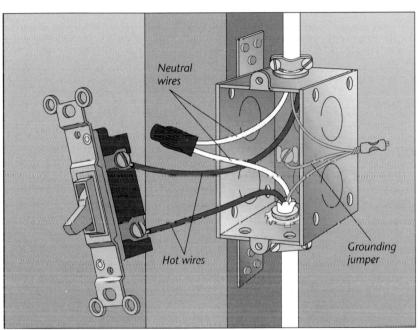

Neutral wires

Hot wires

Grounding jumper

Connecting the new switch

Join the two neutral (white) wires, and screw on a wire nut. Make a grounding connection by bonding the two grounding wires with a compression sleeve or wire nut. If the box is metal, also attach a grounding jumper to the grounding screw in the back of the box. With long-nose pliers form the exposed wire ends of the two hot (black) wires into loops. Wrap them around the screw terminals clockwise and tighten the screws to secure the connection *(above)*.

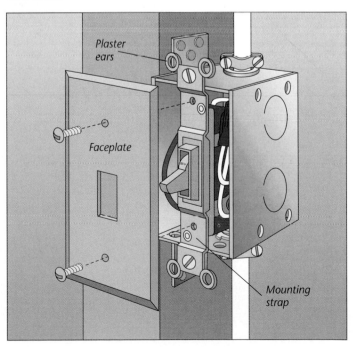

Plaster ears

Faceplate

Mounting strap

Securing the switch

Push the wires and the new switch into the box. Screw the mounting strap on the switch to the box; if necessary, adjust the screws in the mounting slots until the switch is straight. If the switch isn't flush with the wall surface, remove the plaster ears from the mounting strap and use them as shims to bring the switch forward. Screw on the faceplate (in new construction, this is done after the wallboard is in place).

LIGHTING THE OUTDOORS

Electrically, there is no difference between wiring inside and outside—it's the materials that make the difference. Because outdoor wiring must survive the elements, materials are stronger and more corrosion-resistant. Also, everything must fit exactly, so heavy-duty gaskets are often used to seal boxes, thus preventing water from entering them. Shown below, right, are many of the devices that you will need for outdoor wiring projects.

BOXES

Outdoor fixtures come in two types: so-called "driptight" boxes that seal against vertically falling water and "watertight" ones that seal against water coming from any direction.

Driptight: Usually made of sheet metal, driptight boxes often have shrouds or shields that deflect rain falling from above. A typical driptight subpanel is shown at right. This unit is not waterproof and must be mounted where floods, or even "rain" from sprinklers below, cannot touch it.

Watertight: Designed to withstand temporary immersion or sprinkling, watertight boxes are made of cast aluminum, zinc-dipped iron, or bronze, and have threaded entries. All covers for watertight boxes are sealed with gaskets; many of them are equipped with an exterior lever that enables you to operate the switch without opening the cover. The watertight switch box, shown at right, is a typical outdoor box.

GROUND FAULT CIRCUIT INTERRUPTERS

According to present electrical codes, any new outside receptacle (such as one used to plug in a patio charcoal starter or to plug in a radio) must be protected with a GFCI (page 108). To make your job easier when you are tapping into an existing circuit, you can buy a complete kit consisting of a cast aluminum box with cover and a GFCI receptacle.

CONDUIT AND CABLE

Designed to enclose and protect outdoor wiring, conduit shields conductors from moisture and physical harm. Any exposed cable must be covered with some type of conduit. Conduit is sized according to its inside diameter, which ranges from 1/2 inch to 6 inches. The size you need depends on the number and size of conductors the conduit will be holding. Rigid nonmetallic conduit (PVC schedule 40) is the most popular type of conduit and is the first recommendation for any outdoor application. It is lightweight and does not corrode. Connect lengths of PVC conduit by solvent welding to couplings using PVC solvent cement. If covered with a concrete cap, conduit can be buried 12 inches deep. Otherwise, bury it at least 18 inches deep.

Rigid metal conduit is not as popular because it is difficult to assemble. One advantage, however, is that it can be buried at a minimum depth of 6 inches.

Thinwall conduit (EMT) cannot be buried but it is acceptable for vertical runs outdoors. Its advantage over PVC conduit is that it is less expensive and easier to bend. It is generally used along the side of a house or whenever vertical conduit is needed. It must be used with watertight compression fittings.

Underground feeder cable (UF cable) is waterproof, does not require conduit, and can be buried directly in the ground. It's a good idea to cover it with rot-resistant planks before backfilling with soil to protect the cable from being damaged during future digging. This cable, along with some of the conduits discussed above, are illustrated below.

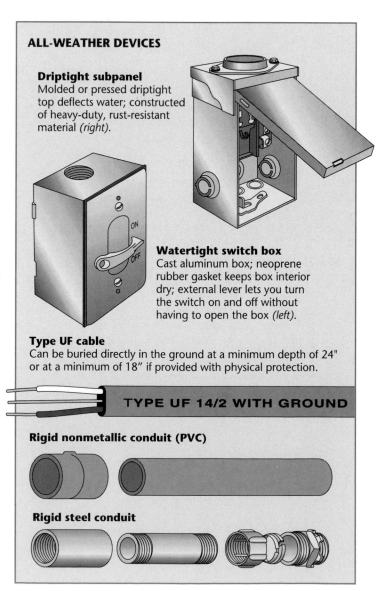

ALL-WEATHER DEVICES

Driptight subpanel
Molded or pressed driptight top deflects water; constructed of heavy-duty, rust-resistant material (right).

Watertight switch box
Cast aluminum box; neoprene rubber gasket keeps box interior dry; external lever lets you turn the switch on and off without having to open the box (left).

Type UF cable
Can be buried directly in the ground at a minimum depth of 24" or at a minimum of 18" if provided with physical protection.

TYPE UF 14/2 WITH GROUND

Rigid nonmetallic conduit (PVC)

Rigid steel conduit

EXTENDING WIRING OUTDOORS

Extending a circuit to the outside of your house requires the same procedures as extending a circuit indoors *(page 92)*. You can tap into existing switch, lighting, and receptacle outlet boxes that are in the middle or at the end of a circuit run.

The four diagrams below show how to extend a circuit outside to a new device. The top two diagrams demonstrate the addition of a watertight extender ring to an existing receptacle *(left)*, and a porch light *(right)*. This extender allows room in the box to wire the new cable, which is run through conduit to the new device.

The bottom two diagrams show how to bring cable outside from inside the house. The easiest way is to install a new watertight receptacle box back-to-back with an existing box in an interior room *(left)*. A hole is drilled through the outside wall, and the cable is fed from the existing box to the new box location. NM cable can be used because the cable is not exposed to the weather. Another option is to tap into a junction box in the attic *(right)* and run cable outside through an LB conduit to a new device. Refer to the diagrams for a list of materials you will need to make the circuit extension.

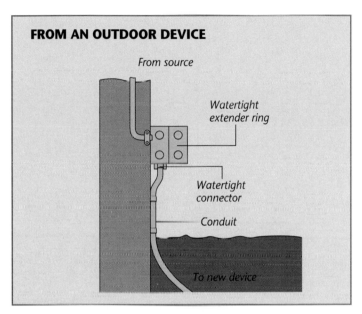

FROM AN OUTDOOR DEVICE

From source

Watertight extender ring

Watertight connector

Conduit

To new device

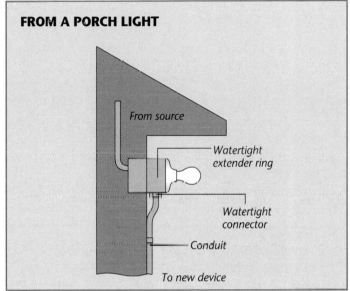

FROM A PORCH LIGHT

From source

Watertight extender ring

Watertight connector

Conduit

To new device

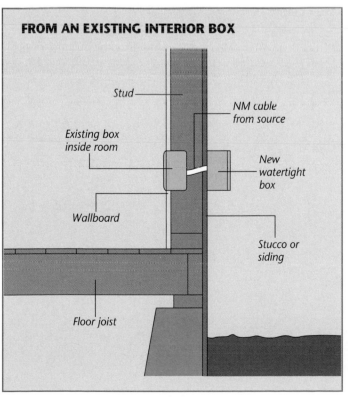

FROM AN EXISTING INTERIOR BOX

Stud

NM cable from source

Existing box inside room

New watertight box

Wallboard

Stucco or siding

Floor joist

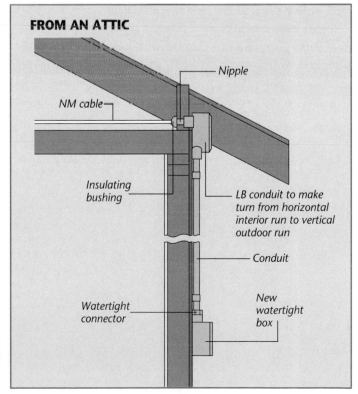

FROM AN ATTIC

Nipple

NM cable

Insulating bushing

LB conduit to make turn from horizontal interior run to vertical outdoor run

Conduit

Watertight connector

New watertight box

Wiring a GFCI Outlet

A ground fault circuit interrupter, or GFCI, is an important safety device which is now required by code for all outdoor electrical outlets as well as for indoor locations where water may be found, such as bathrooms and kitchens. This device works like a standard outlet but cuts off power within ¼₀ second if current begins leaking anywhere along the circuit.

A GFCI can be wired to protect a single location but it can also protect multiple locations by shutting down all devices "forward" of it on the circuit in the event of a leak. Wiring a GFCI is similar to wiring a standard receptacle (page 100) except the terminals are labeled LINE and LOAD. To protect a single location, attach the incoming pair of black and white wires to the terminals at the LINE end. Multiple location wiring is the same for the incoming wires but the outgoing pair of black and white wires attach to the LOAD end.

After wiring an outdoor GFCI, install a gasket in combination with a plastic shield to keep out any moisture. The cover, called a while-in-use cover, flips up to admit a plug.

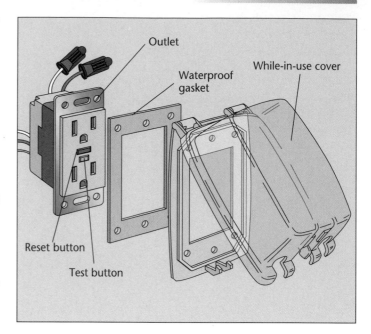

Outlet

While-in-use cover

Waterproof gasket

Reset button

Test button

A 12-VOLT SYSTEM

To install a low-voltage system you'll need a transformer, usually housed in a waterproof box, to step the household current of 120 volts down to 12 volts. Mount the transformer near a watertight switch or receptacle and then run the 12-volt cable a few inches below the ground from the low-voltage side of the transformer to the desired locations for your lights. Burying the cable keeps it hidden and out of the way, but it is acceptable to lay it on the ground and cover it with mulch in a planting area.

A low-voltage system generally comes in a kit with lights, cable, and a transformer. Some light fixtures simply clip onto the wire, others require a clamp connector, while still others must be spliced into the system and connected with wire nuts. Be sure to use the right-sized wire and proper type of connection specified in the instructions. If you don't already have an outlet to plug the transformer into, install a GFCI-protected outlet, as discussed above. If unsure of any wiring aspect, call an electrician.

A typical 12-volt installation Since a 12-volt system uses a greatly reduced voltage, the special conduit and boxes needed for other outdoor wiring are not required. Most transformers are rated for home use from 100 to 300 watts. The higher the rating, the more lengths of 100-foot cable—and consequently the more light fixtures—can be connected to the transformer. Most transformers are encased in watertight boxes; to be safe, plan to install yours at least a foot off the ground in a sheltered area.

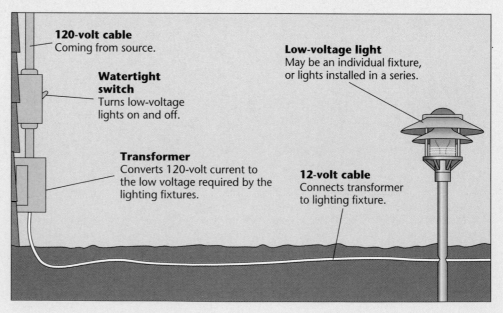

120-volt cable
Coming from source.

Watertight switch
Turns low-voltage lights on and off.

Transformer
Converts 120-volt current to the low voltage required by the lighting fixtures.

Low-voltage light
May be an individual fixture, or lights installed in a series.

12-volt cable
Connects transformer to lighting fixture.

Wiring a Timer

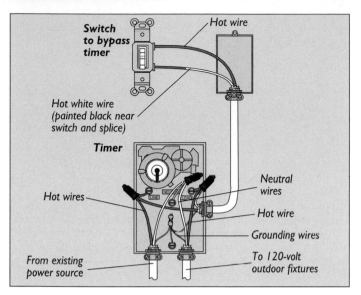

Switch to bypass timer

Hot wire

Hot white wire (painted black near switch and splice)

Timer

Hot wires

From existing power source

Neutral wires

Hot wire

Grounding wires

To 120-volt outdoor fixtures

By wiring in an indoor switch and timer, as shown at left, you can turn outdoor lights on by hand or let the timer turn them on automatically. By wiring the switch to the automatic timer in a switch loop *(page 103)*, the switch can bypass the circuit if you want to turn the lights on or off right away. Connect the incoming black hot wires to the LINE terminal of the timer and the outgoing hot wire and switch wire to the LOAD terminal. Some timers may have wire leaders instead of terminals. Connect the leaders to the wires of the cable with wire nuts. Set the timer according to the manufacturer's instructions.

A 120-VOLT SYSTEM

A 120-volt outdoor lighting system offers several advantages over a 12-volt system. For starters, although 12-volt lights burn more brightly nowadays, light from a single 120-volt fixture can usually illuminate a larger area—especially useful for security and for lighting trees from the ground. A 120-volt system also offers flexibility: power tools, patio heaters, and electric garden tools can also be plugged into 120-volt outlets.

A 120-volt outdoor system consists of a set of fixtures, and either UF (direct burial) 120-volt cable (if allowed by local code) or NM cable in conduit; the length used depends on the size of the wire. Refer to page 107 for some options in extending a circuit outside. You or your electrician will probably connect the system through an indoor switch and timer to an existing electrical source or

circuit, as shown below. You can bury the cable or conduit at a lesser depth if it runs under a concrete walkway.

The diagram shown here will help you understand the basics of installing a 120-volt system. But unless you are well versed in all aspects of electricity you should leave the job to a professional. If you decide to do the installation yourself, remember to shut off the power to the circuit from the service panel *(page 81)* before you start.

120-volt wiring at a glance
The illustration below depicts a standard outdoor wiring setup, using a 120-volt system. The outdoor fixture, housed in the watertight box, is attached by a rigid PVC conduit to the existing indoor circuit structure. If you use UF cable, bury it 24 inches underground, otherwise house NM cable in conduit and bury it at a minimum depth of 18 inches.

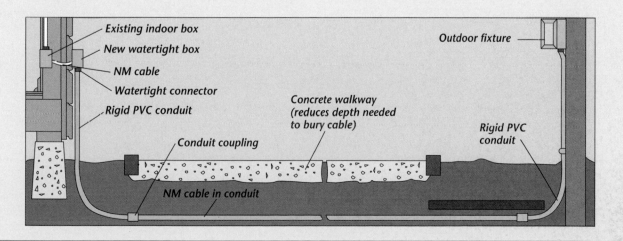

Existing indoor box

New watertight box

NM cable

Watertight connector

Rigid PVC conduit

Conduit coupling

NM cable in conduit

Concrete walkway (reduces depth needed to bury cable)

Outdoor fixture

Rigid PVC conduit

GLOSSARY

Accent lighting
Directed light that illuminates a decorative feature, such as artwork.

Ambient lighting
General room lighting, usually lower light levels than task or accent light; may be direct or diffuse.

Ampacity
Coined word combining ampere and capacity. Expresses in amperes the current-carrying capacity of electrical conductors.

Ampere
Unit used in measuring electrical current, based on the number of electrons flowing past a given point per second. Abbreviated amp. Many wiring system elements are rated in amps for the greatest amount of current they can safely carry.

Branch circuit
Any one of many separate circuits distributing electricity throughout a house from the last over-current device protecting the circuit.

Circuit
Two or more wires providing a path for electrical current to flow from the source through some device using electricity (such as a light) and back to the source.

Circuit breaker
Safety switch installed in a circuit to break electricity flow automatically when current exceeds a predetermined amount.

Color rendering index (CRI)
A measure of how a light source affects the perception of color. Colors appear most natural under light sources with higher CRIs.

Conductor
Technical term for electrical wire.

Conduit
A metal or PVC pipe that is designed to shield conductors from moisture and physical harm.

Correlated color temperature (CCT)
The color appearance of a light source, described in terms of its warmth or coolness. Measured on the Kelvin scale.

Current
Flow of electrons through a conductor; measured in amperes.

Efficacy
A measure, in lumens per watt, of a bulb's or tube's ability to convert electricity into light. More efficacious bulbs produce more lumens for the same number of watts.

Efficiency
A measure of the extent to which a fixture transmits the lumens that its bulbs or tubes emit. More efficient fixtures transmit more of a tube's or bulb's lumens.

Footcandle
A measure of the quantity of light that reaches a surface.

Ground
A conducting body, such as a metal cold-water pipe, that provides electrical current with a path to the ground; sometimes called "grounding electrode." Also, to connect any part of an electrical wiring system to the ground.

Grounding electrode conductor
Connects service panel's neutral bus bar to ground. Sometimes called "ground wire."

Grounding wire
Conductor that grounds a metal component but does not carry current during normal operation. Returns current to source in order to open circuit breaker or fuse if metal component accidentally becomes electrically live.

Hot bus bars
Solid metal bars connected to the main power source in service panel and subpanel. Branch circuit hot wires are connected to them.

Hot wire
Ungrounded conductor carrying electrical current forward from the source. Usually identified by black or red insulation, but may be any color other than white, gray, or green.

Insulation
Material that does not carry current, such as the color-coded thermoplastic insulation on wires.

Joist
Horizontal wooden framing member placed on edge; as in floor or ceiling joist.

Jumper wire
Short piece of wire connected to the electrical box or to an electrical device, such as a switch or receptacle.

Kilowatt
Unit of electrical power equal to 1,000 watts. Abbreviated kw.

Kilowatt-hour
Unit used for metering and selling electricity. One kilowatt-hour equals 1,000 watts used for one hour (or any equivalent, such as 500 watts used for two hours). Abbreviated kwh.

Knockout
Prestamped circular impression in metal electrical boxes that is removed so that cable can enter the box.

Lumen
A measure of the quantity of light emitted by a light source.

Neutral bus bar
Solid metal bar in the service panel or subpanel which provides a common terminal for all the neutral wires. In a service panel, the neutral bus bar is bonded to the metal cabinet and is in direct contact with the earth through the grounding electrode conductor. All neutral and grounding wires are connected to this bus bar. In a subpanel, only neutral wires are connected to the neutral bus bar, which "floats" in the metal cabinet (it is not bonded).

Neutral wire
Grounded conductor that completes a circuit by providing a return path to the source. Except for a few switching situations, neutral wires must never be interrupted by a fuse, circuit breaker, or switch. Always identified by white or gray insulation.

NM cable
A multiconductor consisting of three or more wires contained within the same nonmetallic outer sheathing; used for interior wiring only.

Ohm
The unit of measurement for electrical resistance.

Pigtail splice
The connecting together of three or more wires.

Reflectance
The degree to which surfaces such as walls, ceilings, and floors reflect the light shed on them.

Resistance
Property of an electric circuit that restricts the flow of current. Measured in ohms.

Service panel
Main power cabinet through which electricity enters a home wiring system. Contains main disconnect and grounding connection for entire system; sometimes called a fusebox, panel box, or service entrance panel.

Stud
Vertical wooden framing member; also referred to as a wall stud.

Task lighting
Directed light that illuminates an area where a visually demanding activity takes place; primarily functional.

UF cable
A multiconductor, consisting of three or more wires that are contained within the same non-metallic outer sheathing; used for exterior wiring only.

Volt
Measure of electrical pressure. Abbreviated V.

Voltage
Pressure at which a circuit operates; expressed in volts.

Watt
Unit of measurement for electrical power. One watt of power equals one volt of pressure times one ampere of current. Many electrical devices are rated in watts according to the power they consume. Abbreviated W.

INDEX

ACKNOWLEDGMENTS

Thanks to the following:
AT&T Corp., Parsippany, NJ
Baldwin Hardware Corp., Reading, PA
René Bertrand, Blainville, Que.
City of Stockton Permit Center, Stockton, CA
Centre Do-It D'Agostino, Montreal, Que.
Hydro-Quebec, Montreal, Que.
Kichler® Lighting, Cleveland, OH
Kenneth Larsen, C. Howard Simpkin Ltd., Montreal, Que.
Lamps by Hilliard, Arcata, CA
Lighting Research Center, Troy, NY
Lightolier, Fall River, MA
National Fire Protection Association, Quincy, MA
Nightscaping, A Division of Loran, Inc., Redlands, CA
Edward Devereux Sheffe, New York, NY
Osram Sylvania Products Inc., Danvers, MA
3M Canada Inc., London, Ont.
Joe Teets, Centerville, VA
Walter Tomalty Enterprises Ltd., Montreal, Que.
Underwriters' Laboratories, Melville, NY

*For their valuable contribution to this book,
we would also like to thank each of the lighting
designers, designers, and architects whose work
and ideas are included.*

Picture Credits
p. 4 Philip Harvey
p. 7 Philip Harvey
p. 9 Kenneth Rice
p. 11 *(both)* Philip Harvey
p. 13 Courtesy Lamps by Hilliard
p. 22 Phillip Ennis
p. 25 Philip Harvey
p. 26 Tom Wyatt
p. 27 Philip Harvey
p. 28 *(both)* Stephen Marley
p. 29 Philip Harvey
p. 30 Kenneth Rice
p. 31 Philip Harvey
p. 32 *(both)* Kenneth Rice
p. 33 Philip Harvey
p. 34 Philip Harvey
p. 35 *(upper)* Philip Harvey, *(lower)* Meg McKinney Simle
p. 36 *(upper)* Kenneth Rice, *(lower)* Philip Harvey
p. 37 Kenneth Rice
p. 38 Philip Harvey
p. 39 *(upper)* Emily Minton, *(lower)* Philip Harvey
p. 40 Sylvia Martin
p. 41 *(both)* Philip Harvey
p. 42 *(both)* Philip Harvey
p. 43 Philip Harvey
p. 44 Philip Harvey
p. 45 Philip Harvey
p. 46 *(both)* Russ Widstrand
p. 47 Emily Minton
p. 48 Philip Harvey
p. 49 *(left)* Philip Harvey, *(right)* Tom Wyatt
p. 50 Philip Harvey
p. 51 *(upper)* Philip Harvey, *(lower)* Emily Minton
p. 52 *(left)* Philip Harvey, *(right)* Tom Wyatt
p. 53 Philip Harvey
p. 54 Michael Jensen
p. 55 *(upper)* Meg McKinney Simle, *(lower)* Tom Wyatt
p. 56 *(both)* Philip Harvey
p. 57 Stephen Marley
p. 58 Stephen Marley
p. 59 Philip Harvey
p. 60 *(upper)* Stephen Marley, *(lower)* Philip Harvey
p. 61 Sylvia Martin
p. 62 Jean Allsopp
p. 63 *(upper)* Stephen Marley, *(lower)* Philip Harvey
p. 64 Philip Harvey
p. 65 Philip Harvey
p. 66 *(left)* Philip Harvey, *(right)* Tom Wyatt
p. 67 Philip Harvey
p. 68 *(left)* Philip Harvey, *(right)* Stephen Marley
p. 69 Philip Harvey
p. 70 *(upper)* Jean Allsopp, *(lower)* Sylvia Martin
p. 71 Philip Harvey
p. 72 Philip Harvey
p. 73 *(upper)* Emily Minton, *(lower)* Michael Stokinger